THE GIFT OF
THOMAS JOSEPH WHITE
M.D., L.H.D., F.A.C.P.
TO THE LIBRARY OF
CABRINI COLLEGE
1981

THE MONEY MUDDLE

THE

MONEY MUDDLE

FOR 611

JAMES P. WARBURG

"Our basic trouble is not a money trouble"

NEW YORK · ALFRED · A · KNOPF

1934

TO
THE MEMORY OF
PAUL M. WARBURG
IN THE HOPE
THAT HE WOULD HAVE LIKED
THIS BOOK

Foreword

This book is written with a certain amount of reluctance in the hope that it may be useful.

If what I shall say gives personal offense to any one, I am sorry, for such is not my intention. I am concerned with ideas rather than with people, but ideas personify themselves inevitably in the people who have them.

JAMES P. WARBURG

March 9, 1934
New York City

Contents

THE MONEY MUDDLE

CHAPTER I

Do You Remember?

March, 1933. . . .

In the wheat fields of the Dakotas, the corn fields of Nebraska, and the cotton fields of the South, farmers were getting less for their crops than it cost to raise them. The range lands of the Southwest were dotted with cattle, turned out to forage for themselves, because there would only be further loss in driving them to market.

On railroad sidings, everywhere, locomotives stood in gathering rust, while on way tracks all over the country freight cars waited, their paint blistered and whipped away by summer heat and winter winds of many months of idleness.

Along the Great Lakes, where flows the greatest inland traffic in the world, few ships were moving. In Minnesota and northern Michigan, scarcely a shovel dipped into the rich ore beds of the iron mines along the Vermilion, the Mesabi and Cuyuna ranges and in the districts of Marquette and Negaunee. In the cities, men beat against the closed doors of factories, offering themselves, their bodies, and the sweat of their bodies for anything—ten cents an hour, as many hours as possible—because even a little money meant food and a lien on shelter.

3

Twelve or fifteen—no one knows now just how many million men there were, out of work—they and their families almost a third of the nation's population—waiting for what tomorrow's good fortune might bring, but existing solely on what charity there might be today, wondering if there would be something to eat and if there would be warmth. . . .

And when millions were finding thin comfort in saying: "Things can't be worse," suddenly they were worse.

The entire banking structure collapsed.

Chaos was prevented only because in the previous November a man had gone up and down the country talking about and promising, if elected, a New Deal. And because that man was about to take office, people went on hoping.

Do you remember?

That November landslide, on which Roosevelt came into office, had been not so much a victory for the Democrats as a crushing vote by the people against those who had been in power.

Millions had voted, not for Roosevelt, but against the distress and suffering that had befallen them since the depression started. It was not even a vote against Herbert Hoover, or against the Republicans, so much as a vote against the whole system which had made such things possible. In a sense it was a vote for revolution—or perhaps not for revolution so much as for revolt.

It was a vote that expressed censure on business and political leadership, and revolt against its continuance, but it expressed no desire for a revolutionary change in the form of government or the form of basic economy.

So it was that the stage was set last March for the coming of a great leader. No Barrymore ever had a more effective build-up for his first entrance; and no Barrymore ever played through a difficult first act to more thunderous applause than greeted Roosevelt as the curtain descended upon his first year in office. But, as we go out into the alley to smoke a cigarette during the intermission, let us bear in mind that this is not a one-act play.

Let us remember, in our excitement over the first act, that there are other acts to come, and that the merit of the play cannot be judged until the complicated plot is unravelled further, even though we know at this time that we are witnessing the performance of a great star. But—a great star needs a good supporting cast; and a drama must build, constantly, to its final climax.

And now, before we proceed to review the first act we have just witnessed, let us familiarize ourselves a little with the fabric out of which it was woven.

The first third of this book—Chapters II to XIV—need not concern a reader who is familiar with the general background of money and banking. In these chapters I have sought to provide in simple terms the basic elements of the origin and nature of our money mechanism, and a few simple definitions of much-used and frequently misunderstood terms.

I have done this in order to avoid the necessity of constantly interrupting the story which follows, by pausing here and there to define what this or that term or problem means.

The story that I wish to tell really begins with Chapter XV. It is, as I see it, the story of what we have done since March 1933, why we have done it, and where it leaves us at the present time.

Naturally, opinions differ as to what happened, why it happened, and, most of all, as to what should happen from here on. I shall express my own opinions fully and frankly, avoiding subjects that I know nothing about, and avoiding criticism where I have no constructive suggestion to offer.

The reader must make his or her own allowances for the fact that I am neither an economist nor a politician, but merely a practical banker, who would like to contribute what he can towards the constructive effort of the present and of the future.

PART ONE

A BIT OF BACKGROUND

CHAPTER II

What is Money?

ORIGIN OF COIN AND CURRENCY

Probably there is nothing so universally used and so little understood as money.

What is it? Why do we have it? How is it created? What are its functions, its weaknesses, and its good and bad habits? All these things we ought to know, but we don't. We don't know them because we take the existence of money for granted and concern ourselves solely with getting as much of it as we can, to spend or save, or speculate with, according to our natures.

Money is not the same thing as wealth. Wealth is an accumulation of property, which may be, but need not be, expressed in money.

Money is a medium of exchange. We need it in order that we may trade our work, or the fruits of our work, for the things other people possess that we want. If a workman in a bolt-factory were paid for his labor by being allowed to take home a certain number of the bolts he made each day, he could not get food for his family by offering the grocer bolts in exchange for eggs and vegetables—unless, by chance, the grocer happened to need bolts.

Money is created out of the necessity for some common denominator of value between all the things and services that men have to offer and that other men desire. Since it is needed to perform this function, the primary quality that it must possess is trustworthiness. No one will give up his hours of work, or the things he has produced, in exchange for something concerning the value of which he has any doubts. In other words, the workman would rather take home his bolts and try to get at least a loaf of bread for them than accept his pay in something which might or might not be exchangeable at the grocery store for food in satisfactory quantity.

If money is to be trustworthy, it follows that two general things must be true concerning it:

1. It must be impossible for anyone other than an agreed authority to create it. Otherwise anyone could cheat and simply manufacture for himself all the money he desired without exchanging anything for it.

2. The quantity of money created by the agreed authority must bear a direct relationship to the amount of work done or things exchanged in the community. Otherwise there can be no certainty that a given amount of money will buy a given amount of work or things. This is important. In fact, it is so important that it lies at the root of the whole money question. We shall develop this thought later, but first let us see how money has grown up and changed in the course of history.

As soon as people wanted a medium of exchange, they realized the truth of the first of these requirements for trustworthiness—that is, that it must be impossible for anyone to manufacture himself money. To prevent this they looked around for something that was both durable and rare and yet easy to handle and carry around. That was how they came to select the precious metals as their medium of exchange.

These metals were obtainable out of the ground, but only in limited quantity and after much work and difficulty. Anyone, therefore, who manufactured himself gold or silver by digging it out of the ground was not cheating, because he was producing value for work, just as the farmer who grew potatoes was producing value for work. Potatoes, however, could not serve as money because they were too easy to raise and could be produced in practically any desired quantity. Also they were not durable.

Thus it was that so long as the precious metals constituted the only medium of exchange, the only cheating possible was to attempt to pass off lead for silver, or brass for gold, or to mix in a cheaper metal with a precious one. Very soon, however, there was a new development.

When a man had accumulated a little hoard of gold or silver, by spending less than he earned or through mining or in any other manner, it became impossible to carry it all about with him, and dangerous to leave it lying around. So what did he do? He went to the richest man in the community, who had probably built himself a strong-box, and asked whether he would be good enough to keep the gold for him. The rich man agreed, accepted the gold, gave his receipt for it—and so became the first banker.

Now see what happens. John Thrifty goes home with the signed receipt of Old Strongbox. Pretty soon little

Mrs. Thrifty persuades John that it would be much nicer to own their own house than to have a lot of gold, and, besides, it would save rent. They find the house they want, make their bargain, and John Thrifty shows the other man Old Strongbox's receipt.

The other man says: "Don't bother to get the gold. I don't want it lying around. You come with me to Strongbox and we'll get him to tear up your receipt and give me one instead."

Off they go to Strongbox. But Strongbox, after listening to the story, says: "It's not necessary to write a new receipt. You take Thrifty's receipt, after Thrifty has written his name on it."

That is done, and there we have the first paper money.

In a very short time practically all the gold in the town has found its way into Old Strongbox's strong-box, and the money of the community has become his receipts for gold, issued probably, for the sake of convenience, in round amounts. But that is only the beginning of the story.

Strongbox learns from experience that comparatively few people ever come in to redeem the certificates. For all they seem to care, he might just as well not have enough gold to cover his outstanding receipts. Strongbox is a smart old boy. His chief business has not been the storing of gold—in fact, this is rather a nuisance. His chief business has been money-lending—at a nice fat rate of interest. Hitherto, when he made a loan, that meant that he would give the borrower some of his own gold—on good security of course—and the borrower agreed to bring back the gold on a certain day or else lose his collateral.

Now, however, when a borrower took a loan, Strongbox found that he was quite willing to take a receipt for gold instead of the metal itself. That opened up various possibilities. So far Strongbox's earnings were limited to the interest he could get by lending his own precious metal. What was to prevent his lending some of the other people's gold as well? They would never want it, all at the same time. And now at last Strongbox could see how the gold-storing business could become very profitable!

Further than that, he could not only make interest on his customers' gold as well as his own, but he could do another thing:

He could issue twice as many dollars' worth of receipts as he actually held gold, and thus again double his profits.

Unquestionably Old Strongbox became quite excited over these possibilities. The more he thought about them, the more he saw his great chance. He took it. And there we have the beginnings of a "modernized gold standard" and of a credit system.

Was there anything dishonest about all this?

No. Not dishonest, but risky. There is nothing dishonest in loaning a customer's gold. The customer does not particularly care what Strongbox does with the gold as long as he is prepared to redeem his receipts. But it is dangerous.

Strongbox may make a large loan to a bootmaker, who dies and is shown to be insolvent. And suppose the town gossip makes this loan even larger than it is. What happens? John Thrifty's wife says:

"John, do you suppose our gold is safe with Strongbox?"

"Sure, it's safe," assures John.

"Well, I don't know. I know, of course, that he is awfully rich, but they say he's been losing a lot of money."

But John only smiles. "Don't believe all the things you hear."

"I don't, but—" and the conversation drifts on across the supper dishes, through the evening and into the night, with the result that the following morning John decides to drop in on Old Strongbox "just to take a look around." He finds a number of others "looking around" with the same idea in mind. The uncertainty that began developing the night before comes to a head. He withdraws his gold. And there you have the first panic.

Whether Strongbox can survive it or not depends upon how far fear spreads, how quickly he can call in his loans, and how much of his own gold he has kept unloaned and safe in his strong-box for just such an emergency.

Nor is it dishonest for Strongbox to issue more promises to pay in gold than he actually holds gold, provided he holds against such receipts other assets that are as good as gold. But, again, it is a very risky business. Even more risky than loaning customers' gold, because the temptation is great to overdo it.

In loaning customers' gold Strongbox is limited to the amount of such gold in his possession, but once he starts over-issuing his receipts which circulate as paper money, there is no mechanical limit to stop him. For this reason it did not take long for people to realize that bankers could not be entrusted with the right to create paper money, unless especially authorized to do so under certain rules laid down by the community as a whole. That is why governments took to themselves and jealously guarded the money-issuing power.

But there was a fly in this government ointment as well, as people soon learned to their cost.

A government's revenue comes from duties and taxes. Without revenue no government can maintain an army or a navy or perform any of the functions of preserving law and order. On the other hand, a government exists by the will of the people. Even a tyrant can be a tyrant only so long as the people are willing to put up with him. Therefore it is essential for any government that wants to maintain its power, to maintain the goodwill of the people. Otherwise it can get no money on which to exist. Sometimes it takes generations for a people to rid themselves of the plundering rule of a few, but in the end they succeed. That being so, a government knows that it must keep taxation within bearable limits or else the people will rebel. And now we come to the fly in the ointment.

When a government spends more than its income, it can do three things: it can raise taxes; it can borrow; and it can print money. (It can also go to war and try to seize by force property that belongs to others.) If it raises taxes, it risks its popularity. If it borrows, it must ultimately repay, and that means economizing or raising taxes in the future. If it goes to war, it may lose and be worse off. That is why printing paper money has always been so tempting.

CHAPTER III

Currency Debasement— Government's Temptation

It is important to pause here for a moment and take note of one important thing that happened when governments took for themselves the right to create money.

We have seen how paper money evolved quite naturally out of the necessities and conveniences of life. So long as such money was issued by private bankers, such as Old Strongbox, there was the ever-present danger that bankers would over-extend themselves and that their paper would turn out to be worth less than what it was supposed to be. Periodic experiences of this kind led people to take away this right to create money from individuals and to vest it in themselves—that is, in their government. The way they did this was to declare that only money issued by or for account of the government should be "legal tender." In other words, if you owed a debt and offered to pay it by tendering paper money issued on the government's authority, your creditor would be compelled to accept it in full discharge of the obligation. The creditor could always refuse to accept privately issued money and demand gold, but with the government's money he had no such option.

This legal-tender privilege, of course, gave the government a practical monopoly of the issuance of paper money. But it did something else as well. Whereas the banker was always confronted by the nightmare of a run on his gold supply, which in most cases made him careful not to get over-extended, the government, because of its legal-tender privilege, did not have any such thing to worry about. That is why an extravagant government would be tempted not to cut down expenses, not to increase taxation, not even to borrow and postpone the evil day, but just to print its legal-tender money.

It may not be apparent at first why this is so bad. That is not surprising, because it has taken centuries for people to understand this very problem; and most of them do not fully understand it even today. But it is really quite simple, and, once it is understood, much of the confused thinking and talking about currency inflation is eliminated.

What we must do first is to look at money from a different angle than we have so far. We must look at money as a desirable possession—desirable because it is exchangeable for whatever one wants or needs. From this point of view, when you sell a mule for fifty dollars, you are not so much selling the mule as buying fifty units of the medium of exchange. You are doing this because you want to be able to sell the fifty units in exchange for various other things you may want to possess, more than you want to possess the mule.

You know that each unit of exchange represents a certain amount of gold, and that the amount of gold in the world is limited. You have forgotten, or more likely have never known, just how much gold each unit represents. In fact you have become so used to paper money that you hardly think of it as representing gold, but think of it rather as if it had a value of its own. Most people do this and become so convinced of it that a government which debases its money can fool people into not realizing what is happening for a long time. And that brings us back to our story.

What do we mean when we say that a government debases its currency?

In the old days when there was no paper money, the medium of exchange consisted of metal coins, each containing a certain amount of precious metal. In those days a spendthrift king would replenish his coffers by what was known as coin "clipping"—that is, by snipping off a little bit of each coin, he would collect enough metal to enable him to recoin the melted clippings and thus pay his expenses for a while. So long as this was not detected, nobody cared. Coin "sweating"—melting off a bit—was another favorite method. Just as you and I have forgotten how much gold there is in the dollar (until recently!), so people in those days scarcely thought of weighing gold coins before accepting them in payment. Sooner or later, however, the secret would out, and people would suddenly discover that they had been cheated. Then what happened?

Suppose the King had reduced the weight of the coinage by ten per cent. Suppose I owed you ten dollars and offered you ten debased coins. What would you do?

You would say: "Nothing doing. You owe me so and so many grains of gold, and these ten dollars only weigh ninety per cent of that. So give me another dollar or else give me the actual gold."

Then there would be an argument. I would protest that I hadn't snipped the coins and had taken them as full value. You would say that was my tough luck. And so on. The same thing would re-enact itself all over the country, with the result that all of us would be very angry at the King.

And if we got angry enough, off would come the King's head—or someone else's head. And that would be that.

But when the medium of exchange becomes legal-tender paper money, it is not quite so simple. For one thing, you can't tell by weighing a dollar bill whether it represents the proper amount of gold or not. And, for another thing, these paper dollars are legal tender, so that if you suspect that they are not worth full value, you cannot say to me, as you did of the debased coins: "These ten dollars are worth only nine, so give me another."

If you say that, I shall simply ask you to read what it says on the face of the bill. And, what is more, I shall ask you what makes you think these ten dollars are worth only nine.

That brings us to the heart of the matter. How do you know—how does anybody know—when paper money is being debased? There is, of course, a long and scientific answer to this question, but that belongs in a long and scientific book, which this is not. There is also a very simple practical answer.

You know that a paper currency has become debased whenever people begin to wonder whether it has become debased or not. Usually when that happens, when people begin to be afraid of paper money, the money has already lost a great deal of its supposed value; because debasement is an insidious thing that creeps up before a person really becomes aware of it. There is a perfectly good danger signal. In fact, there are two, but the average man pays very little attention to them.

One danger signal is a *general* rise in prices.

If the prices of two or three things go up, that may be due to a shortage of those things or to a suddenly increased demand for them. But if foodstuffs, coal, clothing, and particularly the raw materials like wheat, cotton, copper, rubber, and sugar, all go up at once, that is a danger signal. You can see why very easily.

Wheat might go up because of a small crop. So might cotton. So might sugar. But it is hardly likely that you would have bad weather for wheat in the Middle West, bad weather for cotton in the South, and bad weather for sugar in Cuba all at the same time. And, so far as I know, there is no bad weather for copper, nor for a lot of other raw materials. Therefore, if all these things "go up," it may be because of increased business and demand, but also they may not be "going up" at all because *money may be going down*. In other words, the prices of all these things in terms of money are going up, which means that the price of money, in terms of everything that money can be sold for, is going down. But that still does not tell us what makes money go down. We shall come to it a little later.

The second danger signal is even more simple, but it is

much more remote from everyday life. It is to be found in the government's budget figures.

Some countries do not publish very clear accounts of their income and expenses. Our Government does. What these figures tell you is whether the government is spending more or less than it is receiving in revenue. If it is spending less, everything is in order. If it is spending more, that is a danger signal. Another way of getting at the same thing is to compare the total government debt in any one year with the same figure in preceding years. If the debt is rising, the government is spending more than it receives. If the debt is falling, the government has been living within its income.

A rapidly increasing debt over a period of years is an unfailing danger signal, but the absence of this budgetary red flag is not a sure sign that there is no danger of money going down. That is because our money is not all Government money. By far the largest part of it is "bank money," in the shape of bank deposits. That is also something to which we shall return later.

CHAPTER IV

Why Government Needs a Nurse

THE CENTRAL BANK

Coming back now to the days when governments first took for themselves the right to issue more paper money than they had gold and of making such money legal tender, let us see what happened when the privilege was abused.

The first thing that happened was exactly the same thing that took place with Old Strongbox. People began to be afraid that there was not enough gold to go around, so they went to the government agency to redeem their paper money. At first the government paid out gold as fast as it was demanded, but sooner or later, if the run kept up, it would see all its gold going out into the hands of the people, and then it would call a halt. When Strongbox did that, he was considered broke, and many other unpleasant things besides. His affairs were taken over by the people to whom he owed money and they divided up what was left. But when a government stops paying gold, it is not so crude about it.

The government does not say: "Sorry, I'm busted." It says that, for one nice-sounding reason or another, it "is suspending specie payments." Then nobody can get any gold from the government any more, but everybody still has to take the government's paper money in settlement of all debts. The paper currency has now become "irredeemable."

The result of this action by the government is almost instantaneous. Gold, which everyone wants, goes to a premium over the paper currency. Expressed the other way round, paper currency is immediately worth less gold than its face value calls for, and a paper dollar will buy fewer eggs or cigarettes than a gold dollar. Accordingly, as fast as you get hold of a gold dollar you keep it, and as fast as you get a paper dollar you try to exchange it for gold, or, failing that, for any sort of things that you can use. In a short time gold has disappeared from circulation entirely, because no one will part with it.

The next thing that happens is that prices rise rapidly in terms of paper dollars, because everyone is trying to do the same thing at the same time—that is, get rid of paper dollars in exchange for things. Meantime wages are still being paid in paper dollars, and pretty soon the wage-earner cannot live on what he earns, because his dollars will no longer buy his necessities. Then the government says that all wages must be raised.

That means that the government itself must pay a great deal more in wages to all its employees. That in turn means that the government prints even more money, and the more it prints, the less people trust it, the higher go prices, the more often must wages be increased, and again the more money the government must pay out. And so it goes, round and round in a circle, until finally a newspaper costs ten thousand dollars, and a pair of shoes costs a million.

Eventually paper money becomes completely worthless. No one will sell anything for any amount of it. And then, mysteriously, gold begins to come out of hoarding.

Almost overnight the whole thing is over. Paper money disappears. The government is overthrown. Gold circulates. The new government gets out a new issue of paper money redeemable in gold, the people gradually acquire confidence in it—and the show is ready to start all over again.

But in the meantime what has happened to the people?

All savings have been destroyed. Ninety-nine men out of a hundred are penniless. A few speculators have made their fortunes; bankers, by and large, have managed to survive; but the great mass of the population have nothing left but their ability to start life over again. And if they are too old for that, God help them. Do you wonder that when governments have turned loose the printing presses, the people have turned loose their wrath in revolution?

Is it conceivable that, in a world in which this has happened time and time again, people will still be fooled by the same old tricks of a government that spends more than it receives?

Unfortunately the answer seems to be yes, because the possible variations of the same old game are infinite in number, and people are always willing to believe that this time it is going to be different. But it never is different, except for the fact that slowly and painfully we have accumulated a certain amount of experience and devised a certain number of safeguards, which nevertheless we often neglect to use.

The first thing that people learned from a series of disastrous experiences with paper money was that a political government could no more be trusted with the right to create money than could private interests. Therefore methods were devised to combine government and private enterprise in a new form of semi-governmental authority. In almost all European countries this was done by organizing a central bank, owned partly by the government and partly by the people and operated for the public interest by non-political officials. In this country we tried both extremes and finally came to much the same solution. First we had a bank owned entirely by the government. Then we gave the power to issue money to the national banks—that is, private institutions operating under a federal (as opposed to state) charter. And finally, in 1914, after any number of "government-money panics" and "bank-money panics," we adopted the Federal Reserve System, with its twelve regional banks, privately owned, but run under the supervision of the government-appointed Federal Reserve Board. It is not true, although frequently stated, that the Reserve System is run by and for the benefit of the private banks. It is true that the stock of the Reserve Banks is owned by the member banks of the System, but the member banks receive only a maximum dividend of six per cent.

The second thing we have learned from experience is that if a currency is convertible into gold coin, the issuing authority should never have less than thirty to forty per cent of its outstanding currency in actual gold holdings. So long as there is that much gold "cover" in the vaults, it seems that people will not under normal circumstances ask for it.

If a currency is redeemable only in gold bars (bullion)—a practice which has recently been developed—it will perhaps be safe to reduce the "gold cover" to a somewhat lower figure. If people can redeem their money only in gold bullion, which comes in bars worth several thousand dollars each, they will not so readily ask for such bars as they would for coin. That, incidentally, is the difference between a "gold standard" and a "gold bullion standard."

We shall consider the workings of the various forms of gold standard more fully after we have discussed the creation of "bank money" and the basic elements of capital and credit. We shall then see what "cover" there should be for that part of the currency which is not covered by gold.

CHAPTER V

Check Money — The Banker's Temptation

In the preceding chapters we have discussed briefly how money first came into existence, and how it developed from precious metal to metal coin, from coin to paper, and how paper tends from time to time to become irredeemable paper instead of a gold-standard currency.

Today, however, neither coin nor paper currency is the most important part of our money mechanism. Few people realize that in this country by far the largest part of the money we use is not currency at all, but "check" or "bank" money. It is a curious thing that there are even quite a number of well-known economists who overlook the importance of this fact.

One of the most popular catch phrases of demagogues has always been that there is a scarcity of money, and when they use this argument, almost invariably they talk as if all the money in the country consisted only of currency, without taking into account the billions of bank deposits. It is easy to see that this is nonsense. According to these people, if Mr. Rockefeller has only ten dimes and a five-dollar bill in his pocket, even though he has millions on deposit at his bank, all Mr. Rockefeller's money only amounts to six dollars! Wouldn't he be surprised to learn that?

Since we have some forty billions of money on deposit in banks in this country, as against only about five billions of currency, let us see what sort of money this "bank money" is. The story of its origin is very similar to the story of the origin of paper money.

You will remember how our friend John Thrifty went to Old Strongbox to deposit his gold in exchange for a warehouse receipt, and how that receipt developed into paper money. The same thing happened again when John Thrifty had accumulated more paper money than he was likely to need for some time.

He did not like to carry it around or leave it at home, and because he wanted a safe place to store it, he went again to Old Strongbox, the banker, and asked him to take the currency and give him a receipt. What the banker did in this case was to open an account on his books, in which he entered the fact that on a certain day John Thrifty had deposited the sum of one hundred dollars. Now, when John purchased a cow a little later, he gave Bill Cowboy an order for thirty dollars on Strongbox—that is, he gave Bill a letter to Strongbox, directing the banker to pay the bearer, Bill Cowboy, thirty dollars out of the hundred that John had lying there. This the banker did, entering the amount on Thrifty's account as a deduction, and there you have the first check.

Now suppose that Bill Cowboy also had more cash than he needed, and suppose he asked Strongbox to keep the thirty dollars for him. Then Strongbox would open another account, this time in the name of Bill Cowboy, and he would simply credit this account with the thirty dollars, which he had just deducted from the account of John Thrifty.

The important thing to realize about this transaction is that one man paid another man thirty dollars, and yet no paper or gold money was involved at all. In other words, the payment was made by a transfer of credit on the banker's books; what passed from one man to the other was "bank money."

But that is not the whole story. So far no additional money has been created, because, while all this was going on, Thrifty's original hundred dollars was still lying in the banker's till. But if Old Strongbox left the currency lying in his till forever, there would be no profit for him in all this making of entries. So what does he do? He lends out at interest as much as he dares of the currency deposited with him. Suppose he lends it all out. Then you can see that there has really been created an additional hundred dollars of money that had not existed before. Thrifty has seventy dollars in his account. Cowboy has thirty dollars in his. And the butcher has a hundred dollars in currency, which he has borrowed from Old Strongbox. Do you see what this means? It means that when a banker extends credit, he actually creates money.

But, you may say, suppose Thrifty or Cowboy or both want to draw out their money; if it has been lent to the butcher, how can they get it? The answer is that they can't, if Strongbox has been foolish enough to loan out all the money that has been deposited with him—unless, of course, he can immediately squeeze his money back out of the butcher. Therefore what actually takes place is that the banker always keeps a certain proportion of his depositors' money in actual cash, to be prepared for any normal withdrawals. The rest he lends out to make interest, being very careful to lend it on good security and for short periods of time, so that he can reduce his loans to cash quickly, in case of abnormal withdrawals by his depositors.

When you consider now that we have over forty billions of money created in this way through deposits, as against five billions created by the government in currency, do you see how important "bank money" is?

And do you see how necessary it is that the right to create such money should be jealously guarded, entrusted only to bankers of intelligence and integrity, and subject to strict rules and supervision?

And are you not surprised that in this great country of ours we still have no uniform banking law and are still laboring with an antiquated hybrid banking system?

That is one of the major problems of reform which face us today. We have the Federal Government and forty-eight different states, each making its own banking laws, each with its own rules of operation, and we have not yet brought the power to create "bank money" under anything like intelligent control.

CHAPTER VI

Capital and Credit

When, in a previous chapter, we first considered the origin and basic nature of money, we discovered two essential elements of trustworthiness. The first, with which we have just dealt, concerns the careful guarding of the right to create money; the second is that the amount of money in circulation must always bear the right relationship to the amount of work done or things exchanged in the community.

In order to understand what this means, we must first draw a distinction between money and capital. We have seen that money is a medium of exchange. It would seem to follow, therefore, that the amount of money in circulation would depend, first, upon the amount of things or services that are being exchanged; and secondly upon the rapidity with which the medium of exchange circulates.

You can readily see that the same dollar bill can serve as a medium by which several exchanges of goods are made in one day. Accordingly it is not necessary to create as much money as one would at first suppose. It is only necessary that there be enough money in relation to the turnover of things so that, moving around busily during the day, money will go to bed each night having done all the work that there was to be done.

Now, however, we come to a new problem. Everyone who receives money in payment for work uses such money in the first instance to pay for what he must consume. But if all incomes were consumed completely in this way, the production of goods would very soon come to a standstill.

This is true because the production of goods requires not only labor, but capital, in the shape of factories, tools, machines, transportation, and so forth. This capital, moreover, is constantly being consumed. The average life of some factory equipment, for instance, is only five to ten years. Therefore money is required not only to maintain these fixed elements of production, but also to increase the output of goods required by an increasing population and a progressively improving standard of living. Since this is so, a certain amount of the money income of the population must constantly be withheld from consumption, in order to create the capital needed to make production possible.

That is what happens when people set aside savings accounts or buy bonds or mortgages or shares. They are putting a part of their money to work in the processes of production. The farmer who buys a plow is doing the same thing, only he does it direct. The man who puts his money in a savings bank or in life insurance does it indirectly, because he enables the savings bank or insurance company to buy bonds or mortgages, which are a loan that enables someone else to acquire the fixed assets necessary for production.

So we see that not only is money necessary to convert hours of labor into food and clothing, but that a certain amount of it must constantly accumulate into capital. The means by which this accumulated capital finds its way into the channels of production is what we call the credit and investment machinery. And here it is very important that we take note of one fact and hang on to it.

Credit cannot create money for capital investment.

The credit machinery can only direct the flow of capital into productive investment, but the capital must be there—it must have been created, or be in the process of creation, by savings out of incomes. Credit can, and frequently does, anticipate the creation of capital, but when it does so, the capital it creates "out of the air" will again vanish into the air, if the anticipated savings do not materialize.

Let us illustrate this, because it is basically important.

A shoemaker has been making shoes by hand and earning a decent living. The population of his village has grown so that he cannot make as many shoes as he could sell. He wants to install certain machinery, but lacks the capital—that is, has not saved the money—to buy the machinery. On the other hand he figures that with the new machine he can double his earnings and in six months pay for the equipment. He goes to the banker and tells his story. The banker has in his charge the savings—that is, the capital—of others.

The story sounds reasonable, and the banker makes the loan at six per cent interest. Now, if the anticipated earnings materialize and the shoemaker sets them aside according to schedule, he will repay the loan with interest in six months. That means that he will have created the capital he needed out of the anticipated earnings, and the banker's capital is now free to help someone else do the same thing. Furthermore it has increased by three per cent.

If, on the other hand, the machine turns out to be a disappointment, or people don't like the shoes it makes, or another shoemaker comes to town who makes better shoes, then the borrower will not make his anticipated earnings. He will not be able to repay his loan. The bank loses its money, because it can neither use nor sell the machine, and the credit which created capital "out of the air" again vanishes into the air. The same thing is true if people buy worthless stocks, or mortgages on unprofitable farm or real-estate developments.

Thus we see that upon the banker rests another responsibility.

He not only creates money as a medium of exchange, but he also directs the flow of capital into the channels of production. If he does his work well, the community prospers (assuming there are no other disturbances to its economic life), and if he is careless or unintelligent—not to mention dishonest—the whole community suffers from retarded production and diminished savings. These in turn express themselves in high living costs and diminished incomes.

CHAPTER VII

Commercial Paper as Backing for Paper Money

One of the things we have learned from experience and gradually incorporated into our banking practice is to distinguish between the financing of self-liquidating transactions, and other transactions. Bankers have learned that it is far safer to finance an importation of a staple commodity, such as sugar or wool, which is to be consumed or manufactured, than to finance the building of a new shop. The one is a loan which pays itself off as the merchandise is sold, whereas the other must be liquidated out of general profits. The one might be called financing goods in the process of consumption—that is, turnover—whereas the other is a capital loan. It is reasonably safe for a bank to invest a part of its depositors' money in turnover loans, which are commonly called "commercial paper," but it is dangerous to invest depositors' demand money in capital loans. The latter should be obtained through the mortgage or investment market.

Out of this distinction there arises a most important element in the whole structure of "bank money." Central banks have come to put a premium on "commercial paper," by being willing to lend private banks at a low rate of interest on their holdings of such paper. This is what is called rediscounting by the Central Bank, and this practice assures the private banker that he can at all times get cash on such loans, in the event of withdrawals by depositors in excess of his own cash reserves.

The rate at which the Central Bank is willing to refinance the private banks, and which is fixed from time to time by the Central Bank authorities, is known as the "rediscount rate" or sometimes just as the "bank rate." The fixing of this rate is in normal times what determines the level of interest rates for the whole country. It is easy to see why, because the banker, realizing that he may have to borrow, will automatically base his charges to his customer upon the figure fixed by the Central Bank. If the Central Bank is going to charge four per cent for rediscounting, the banker will leave himself a leeway of at least a half per cent over that rate. Therefore even his best customers will have to pay four and a half per cent, and the more risky loans will range above that figure.

When a private banker rediscounts with the Central Bank, he must guarantee the loans he refinances by endorsement. The Central Bank then makes available the actual cash or gives him a corresponding credit on its books. If it pays out cash, it thereby increases its outstanding issue of paper money. If it gives the private banker a book credit, it increases its deposit liability. In either case it holds, as an offset to the newly created liability, commercial paper of short maturity with the endorsement of the private banker.

Out of this type of transaction there arises the cover for that part of a central bank's note-issue (paper money) which is not covered by actual metal.

In other words, what we have learned through bad experience with paper money is to limit its issue by central banks not only to a certain percentage of gold cover, but to the financing of self-liquidating transactions by that part of the note-issue which is not covered by gold.

What we are still in the process of learning in regard to "bank money" (although bad experience should long ago have taught us) is to limit its creation more strictly to the financing of turnover, and to leave to the investment market the supplying of capital funds.

With these things in mind we can now proceed to consider the relation between the supply of money and capital and the price structure.

CHAPTER VIII

Money and Prices

ENOUGH MONEY OR TOO LITTLE?

The question of the relation between money and prices is a favorite battle-ground of economists and politicians. Volumes have been written on the subject, and to attempt to treat the matter here in a brief chapter is to invite all sorts of criticism from the learned brotherhood.

But we are not concerned here with the so-called initiated nor with their criticism. We are concerned here with an attempt to give the uninitiated a working knowledge of the problem. This is not easy to do, because practice and theory are in this instance fairly well interwoven, and we are seeking throughout to avoid theory and stick to practice. Let us see what we can do.

Prices of things are expressed in money, because, as we have seen, money has been made the common measure of value. If there is a scarcity of certain things, prices of those things go up, when there is more competitive demand for them. Similarly, if there is too great an abundance of things, the prices of such things go down, because there are more people trying to exchange them for money than there are people trying to exchange money for those things. That much, I think, we all know. But here is where we come to the more obscure part.

Just as demand and supply govern the relative prices of things, so also demand and supply govern to a certain extent the *price of money*. By "price of money" we mean its price in terms of things—in other words, its purchasing power. If there is a great "plenty of money," prices of things tend to rise in terms of money, which is the same as saying that the price of money tends to go down. In the same way, when money is "scarce," its purchasing power tends to rise—which means that the prices of things tend to go down, and the price of money tends to rise. That may sound complicated, but it really is not, and if you have understood it, the worst is behind you.

You may have noticed that I have put quotation marks around "plenty of money" and around "scarce." You may have noticed also that I have said that the price of money *tends* to rise or fall—not just "rises" or "falls." This is important. Without these distinctions you have what is known as the pure "quantity theory of money."

According to this theory, if you double the amount of money, you reduce its purchasing power by half; if you halve the amount of money, you double its purchasing power. In actual practice, however, it does not work that way.

The mere fact that there is a certain amount of money— let us say a hundred thousand dollars—in the community, does not mean that this whole quantity of money has any direct effect on prices. Suppose, for example, that there is one rich man in the community, who has fifty thousand dollars put away in his strong-box, and that he has no desire to do anything with these idle dollars except to keep them safe. Then, although there are a hundred thousand dollars in the community, only half of this amount is in circulation, and, so far as prices are concerned, the other fifty thousand dollars might just as well not exist.

We see, therefore, that "plenty of money" or "scarcity of money" does not mean the amount of money that there is in a given community, but rather the amount of money that there is in circulation. But that is not all.

The important thing about money in its effect on prices is the frequency with which it is used to facilitate an exchange of goods or services. If a rich man's money in a strong-box is not used at all, it has no effect. Similarly, fifty thousand dollars being used twice a day by the community normally has the same effect on prices as a hundred thousand dollars being turned over only once a day.

Thus "plenty of money" or "scarcity of money" is not caused solely by the amount in circulation, but may be due to the rapidity with which it circulates. That is why the pure "quantity theory of money" is misleading.

The rapidity of circulation depends upon the desire of people to exchange goods for money or money for goods—in other words, it depends upon the state of trade. Good business means more turnover, bad business less. Good business therefore means more rapid circulation of money, and steadier or higher commodity prices. Bad business means reduced circulation and unstable or lower commodity prices.

In the last analysis, unless money is debased, it is the

state of mind of a community that determines the purchasing power of its money, rather than the quantity of money in existence, because the state of mind of the people determines the velocity of circulation. There *can* be an actual scarcity of money. The supply can actually be so small that the amount of money in existence cannot get around fast enough to keep up with the desire of people to exchange goods and services. When that happens, prices may be depressed by an actual "scarcity of money"; but that is never the case when there is "plenty" of idle money lying around in banks and strong-boxes, as there is in this country today.

We have at present hundreds of millions of idle dollars, piled up and doing nothing, because there is not enough business being done to make these dollars go to work and circulate.

That is why, when the demagogue talks about a "famine of money," he is talking nonsense. We have no famine of money. We are just now suffering from a condition which makes those who have wealth afraid to risk it for the sake of getting more.

The chance of profit is momentarily obscured by the fear of loss.

That "state of mind" on the part of those who have—even though it be justified—makes it difficult and sometimes impossible for those who have not to obtain any money at all. Therefore it very reasonably seems to the man in distress that there is a "famine of money." It is small consolation to tell him that there is "plenty of money" and that he is suffering from "a state of mind of the community." And yet that is true. Creating more idle money will only aggravate the trouble.

But a "state of mind" is not just an arbitrary whim. It reflects things that have happened as well as things that are expected to happen. It reflects desires, ambitions, hopes, and fears. It reflects experiences of the past and habits that have accumulated out of experience.

If we follow the demagogue and increase the supply of money, all we shall do is to pile up more idle money, unless something else is done to increase the volume of business.

Anything in the nature of experimentation with money disturbs confidence and drives wealth from working for the public good into hiding. When wealth hides, the poor suffer more than the rich.

Whether it is right that there should be "rich" and "poor" to the extent that we have them in this country is a basic question of philosophy, which has nothing to do with the subject of this chapter. We cannot hope to have an equal distribution of wealth, because, as we have seen, there must always be a constant accumulation of capital to provide the tools and machinery of production. We can, I think, do certain things to prevent too great a concentration of wealth in the hands of a few, but we shall come to that later.

The point of this chapter is:

That increasing the quantity of money, when there is excess idle money, will not relieve suffering, will not redistribute wealth more equitably, will not in fact do anything —except pile up more idle money.

On the other hand, if money is debased for the sake of

increasing the quantity, it not only will fail to help, but will injure the majority of the people.

The thing that will help is to get more money into more active circulation. That cannot be done by tinkering with money itself. It can only be done by removing those factors which today obscure the hope of reasonable return from work and enterprise. Once those factors are removed, business will pick up, employment will increase, and, as wages and profits rise, more and more of the idle dollars will move faster and faster into circulation.

Then there is a healthy adjustment of prices.

I do not want to complicate this chapter by going into too much detail, but I cannot leave it as it stands without adding one general statement:

In our present-day money structure we have metal, paper currency, and bank deposit or "check money." In applying the price theory briefly and perhaps rather dogmatically stated in this chapter, one must of course apply it to the sum total of all the various kinds of money in circulation. It is the quantity of all kinds of money in circulation and the velocity with which it circulates that determines the price level. To apply the theory merely to gold, as some do, or merely to currency, is to miss the point altogether.

CHAPTER IX

The International Aspect

THE GOLD STANDARD

So far we have considered money purely from the internal point of view. If there were only one country in the world, we need go no further. But that is not the case. For various reasons, some racial, some geographical, and some political, there are a number of nations in the world, each with its own monetary system and its own economic individuality. If each nation were completely self-sufficient, then the question of money would be one for each country to settle within its own borders. But that also is not the case.

For instance, Brazil until very recently produced very little except coffee and the bare necessities of life. If Brazilians wanted automobiles or machinery or any number of manufactured articles or luxuries, they had to import them. Importing means buying from another country, and to do that you have to be able to pay the other country. So Brazil exchanged its surplus coffee for the things it wanted to import.

A country like England, on the other hand, does not produce nearly enough of the necessities of life to take care of its own population. For centuries England has been an importer of foodstuffs and raw materials. She pays for these purchases abroad chiefly in two ways: by manufacturing raw materials into finished goods which are wanted by countries like Brazil, and by being the world's great transportation company. "Britannia rules the waves" has more than a political significance. By fetching and carrying goods from and to all parts of the world for other nations, Great Britain has earned in freight charges much of the money she needs to pay for her imported foodstuffs.

From what we have seen in the preceding chapters concerning the accumulation of capital out of savings, it is obvious that to do what Great Britain does requires a great deal of capital and could only be done by a nation that had been accumulating savings for many years.

The textile plants in Lancashire, which take our raw cotton and make it into clothes for the Chinese and Indians, cost a lot of money to build and to keep up. The great fleet of ships that fly the British flag likewise represent a huge capital investment. But this is an investment that has paid for itself many times over. It was due to British sailors in British ships that the Union Jack was planted in all the choice spots of the earth. The British Navy was what enabled England to seize and hold for herself a vast colonial empire, from which she could derive the foodstuffs and raw materials that she needed. All this would have been impossible if the British people had not for years and years been putting aside capital out of their incomes.

And it goes even further. The accumulations of British capital were so great that there was much left over after the plants and ships were taken care of—so much that Great Britain became the banker for the world. British capital flowed into the development of foreign countries, built railways in South America, developed gold mines in Africa, and rubber plantations in the Far East. The result of this investment abroad was that another source of income was added to the British international budget, for the interest on these investments again constituted an offset to the British purchases abroad.

At this point let us fix firmly in our minds two terms that are constantly confused with each other, and then we shall have less difficulty in understanding the international aspect of money. These terms are:

1. "Trade Balance";
2. "Balance of Payments."

A country's trade balance is simply the difference between the sum total of all its imports and the sum total of all its exports. If the imports are greater, the amount by which they exceed the exports constitutes what is known as an "unfavorable trade balance." In other words, the country is buying more abroad than it sells. If the sum of the exports is greater, the amount by which exports exceed imports constitutes a "favorable trade balance."

The "balance of payments," on the other hand, is less easy to visualize. It consists first of all of the "trade balance," but to it must be added the so-called "invisible" items. These are the very type of things we have just been discussing in the case of England, such as freight charges and interest on investments abroad. Thus a country might have an unfavorable trade balance, and still have a favorable balance of payments, because the deficit of exports as against imports would be more than wiped out by the net balance of "invisible" receipts.

In the opposite case, a country whose exports show a favorable balance over imports might end up with an unfavorable balance of payments if, for instance, it had a very heavy interest charge to meet on loans contracted abroad. Germany after the War is an excellent example.

All this digression into international trade was necessary so that we might intelligently approach the international aspect of the money question.

If a country's balance of payments were to come out exactly even, there would of course be no need for any method of settlement. Such, however, is practically never the case.

For one thing, even if the sum total shows neither plus nor minus, the sum total is composed of a series of debit balances with one group of countries and a series of credit balances with others. There is no way in which these can be matched off without some machinery of settlement. For another thing, the items which compose the whole picture are only to a very small extent transactions entered into by the governments themselves.

The bulk of international payments arises from transactions between private individuals or concerns in one country and similar concerns or individuals in other countries. Therefore a government cannot forecast very accurately what the immediate balance of payment will look like, though it can to a large extent control its long-run character.

The methods of control available to governments are, generally speaking, economic and financial. By raising its import duties a country can usually reduce its imports, particularly imports of luxuries and semi-luxuries. By lowering them it can produce the opposite effect. Export bounties, quotas, immigration restriction—these are all economic methods of controlling the movement of goods and services between nations.

The financial means of regulation consist chiefly in making money cheaper or dearer and in stimulating or restricting foreign lending. To see how these methods work we must first understand the operation of an international monetary standard.

Inasmuch as international payments must constantly be made, as we have seen, it follows that there must be a means of payment. If one international super-bank issued all the money for the world, the problem, from this particular point of view, would be somewhat simplified. Such an international money some day will probably exist, but that is a development for which the world is certainly not ready today. Therefore, since different nations will insist on each having its own money, we have the problem of how to measure the value of all these moneys in terms of each other. That is all that the mysterious term "foreign exchange" really signifies.

Once again, just as money originated from the need of a common denominator for goods and services within a community, so we have the need of a common denominator between one nation and another. And, once again, for precisely the same reasons that led us to use the precious metals at home, we came to use them as an international measure of exchange values. Originally both gold and silver were used. For various reasons, which we shall treat separately under the heading of silver, the white metal was gradually discarded as an international yardstick. In order to simplify this particular aspect of our discussion, let us leave aside the question of bimetallism entirely.

Gold came to be used as the international measure through a very simple development. The British chose as their unit of exchange the pound sterling. Originally this actually meant a pound weight of silver. As gold came into use, a number of grains of gold were designated as being equivalent to a pound of silver. Later, when silver was discarded, the pound sterling became merely a name for so and so many grains of gold, which had once equalled a pound of silver.

In other nations the story was much the same. Each adopted, for its own sometimes quite arbitrary reasons, a unit of exchange equivalent to a certain number of grains of precious metal. Now, if it so happened that we adopted as our unit the dollar, equivalent to a little more than one fifth of the amount of gold contained in the British pound, it would follow quite of itself that a pound would be worth a little less than five dollars. The exact figure happened to be $4.8667.

That is all there is to the history of the first exchange parities; they were simply a translation of one currency into the terms of another by means of gold. It was therefore quite natural that when paper money came in and was redeemable in gold in the same units as the original gold coinage, paper money too should be translated back and forth in the same terms.

And now we come to the really interesting part.

Suppose that in a certain country prices have risen. The result would be that this country could sell less of its expensive things to other countries where prices had not risen, and would begin to import more, because its merchants would find it cheaper to buy abroad. The consequence of that would be a great demand for foreign money with which to buy abroad, and a small supply of foreign money because of the smaller proceeds of exports. As always when demand exceeds supply, the price of foreign money would therefore rise.

But we must remember that both at home and abroad the central banks are obligated to redeem their paper money in gold. Therefore, when the price of foreign money rises, it becomes cheaper for the domestic merchant to redeem his paper money in gold and ship the actual gold abroad in payment of his bills than to pay the higher price for foreign money. If we have got that clear, we have got to the essence of the whole gold-standard mechanism.

In actual practice the banks do not wait for the merchant to come and get his gold for shipment abroad. The cost of shipping gold to each country is an established fact, and the banks know that when the exchange rate (the price for foreign money) of that country reaches what is known as the "export point," gold will start to move to that country.

When the "export point" is reached, the banks ship gold to the other country and thereby hold down the price of that country's money.

Exactly the same thing works the other way round. When prices fall in a given country, exports increase and imports diminish. Therefore the price of foreign money becomes less and foreign merchants have to pay in gold to avoid loss, which means that the foreign banks ship gold. That is how the flow of gold automatically keeps the exchange rates between countries on the gold standard from fluctuating by more than the cost of shipping metal.

And now we see the importance of understanding about the trade balance and the balance of payments. Obviously the Central Bank cannot go on giving up gold for shipment very long to make up for an unfavorable balance of payments. If it goes on shipping, sooner or later it will endanger the safety of its currency, for it must not allow its stock of gold to fall below the 30–40 per cent danger line.

There is no way in which a Central Bank can control the balance of payment. All it can do is to take certain measures which will offset temporary disequilibrium, and ship gold until equilibrium is re-established. A country with a continuous unfavorable balance of payment is automatically forced to suspend the gold redemption of its currency. That is what happens when a country is "forced off gold." To prevent such a development requires not only an intelligent tariff policy so as to regulate imports and exports— that is, the trade balance—but intelligent control of credit at home to prevent a violent rise or fall of prices, and intelligent control of foreign lending and borrowing. The latter factor, while not directly affecting the trade balance, does directly affect the total balance of payment.

What a Central Bank can and should do is this:

To begin with, it should constantly be studying all the available material concerning the various items that go to make up the balance of payments. It should know what are the signs of a definite trend, and what are merely seasonal fluctuations, due to crop movements and the like. Whenever a definite unfavorable trend becomes manifest and threatens to cause considerable losses of gold, the Bank should at once raise its rediscount rate and attempt to restrict credit.

The effect of such action is twofold. In the first place, raising the rate makes money dearer. Fewer can afford to borrow; business falls off; and prices tend to fall. In the second place, if fewer borrow, then fewer bankers rediscount, and that means a contraction of the amount of money outstanding, which makes the ratio of the Central Bank's gold holdings to its outstanding currency that much safer. By these and other means (open market operations) too technical for this discussion, but of the same general nature, a Central Bank can by prompt and intelligent action ward off many a storm.

The trouble in the past has been not so much a lack of intelligence on the part of the Central Bank officials as the fact that to check rising prices—that is, a boom—is a very unpopular undertaking. In fact it is so unpopular that political governments will all too frequently bring pressure to bear upon their Central Bank to prevent the very action that should be taken. This is because people in general do not understand that a boom must lead to the consequences we have just seen.

Another trouble has been that there has been in practically all countries a completely inadequate control both of foreign borrowing and of foreign lending. We need only look at the German orgy of post-war borrowing and our own orgy of post-war lending to see the evil consequences of excess in either direction.

And, finally, we must not forget that our monetary machine, which is now so often blamed for all our troubles, broke down more than ten years *after* the rest of civilization broke down—after we indulged in all the follies and waste of a World War and all the inanities of an economically impossible peace.

There is much that can be improved in our money mechanism, much that we can learn from our recent experiences, but before we construct a new system, let us be sure that we understand the old.

CHAPTER X

Who Killed Cock Robin?

WHAT HAPPENED TO THE GOLD STANDARD

For quite a number of years prior to the War the gold standard had been functioning smoothly and effectively. And after the War it seemed for a time as if an international gold standard would again be generally adopted; in fact it took ten years of economic chaos to throw the majority of nations off gold. It is not difficult to understand what happened.

In the first place the War brought about terrific governmental expenditure on the part of the participating nations. What is more, these expenditures were mostly for destructive purposes. If you and your neighbor each have a house and a thousand dollars, and you each spend your thousand dollars for dynamite to blow up each other's houses, the financial condition of both of you will scarcely benefit by the experiment. That is exactly what the warring nations did. Only they spent more money than they had. They went deeply into debt as well. As a result, when the War was over, all the nations that had been in it were struggling under a load of interest charges, to meet which they had to raise taxes or print money.

In the second place, the whole machinery of production

was thrown out of kilter, not only in the warring nations, but in many neutral countries. Millions of men left their peace-time occupations and became soldiers. Millions of other men and women became civilian war workers. Certain industries were enormously stimulated to supply the necessities of warfare; others ceased to operate. Some prices went crazily up, and others crazily down.

Then, suddenly, after four years, the War was over, and all this shifting of lives had to be done over again. Millions of soldiers came back and wanted their old jobs. If they got them back, war workers became unemployed; if the soldiers did not get their jobs back, they had difficulty finding employment. Industries had come to use women workers in many places where they had formerly employed men. In addition, the war industries themselves were now largely without work and had to change to peace-time production.

All this meant that unemployment became the great social problem. If a government did nothing to relieve the jobless, it ran the certain danger of unrest and disorder. If, on the other hand, a government wanted to help, where was it to get the money? Most governments adopted some form of dole, and in addition many of them embarked on programs of public works expenditure for the purpose of creating jobs.

When they did this, the governments had to raise taxes. When taxes were raised, industry and trade became less profitable, with the result that the employer who had barely been making both ends meet could no longer do so. That, in turn, threw more people out of work, and the government had to spend still more money to support the unemployed. There you have the typical deflationary spiral, which is accompanied by less and less turnover, less and less production, and consequently less and less money in circulation. Do you recognize it?

During such a period the demagogues blossom forth, and their invariable cry is for more and cheaper money. One might just as well ask for more gasoline in the tank of an automobile that has broken its crank-shaft.

In the third place, in addition to unbalanced budgets and unemployment, there was the complete dislocation of international trade and finance. Under the impetus of war all countries tried to become as nearly self-supporting as possible. Particularly did they try to grow their own foodstuffs. Now, if a country like Germany wants to grow its own wheat, and if it is more expensive to grow wheat in Pomerania than in Nebraska, the inevitable result is that Germany will erect a tariff wall to keep out the cheaper wheat from abroad. The result is that the Germans have to pay more for their bread, and the American wheat farmer loses his export market.

But it goes much further than that. Countries with adverse balances of payment set out to reduce their imports by all sorts of restrictions on trade, and at the same time they were trying to increase their exports. One need only realize that one country's imports are another's exports to see where this leads.

Added to all this there was the Treaty of Versailles, with its impossible burden of Reparations on Germany, and the creation of a lot of new political entities, each with its own problems of economic existence. And on top of all that there were the war debts, owed in the last analysis to America, and impossible to pay back to America so long as America has a favorable balance of payments.

There was the post-war picture. Now see what happened.

In some countries—Germany and Austria—the resistance broke. The cry for more and cheaper money, for more and more government spending, carried the day, with the result of complete and total currency inflation. In those countries savings were destroyed. The middle class was wiped out, and the whole social structure overturned. A few rich speculators, such as Stinnes or Castiglioni, emerged with enormous fortunes; a few others managed to save a little out of the wreckage; but the rank and file of the population were literally penniless.

In other countries, such as France, Belgium, and Italy, the same process started, but was arrested short of ultimate disaster—not, however, without acute misery and suffering.

When a country goes through complete inflation of its currency as Germany did, to the point where the currency has become literally worthless, it thereby wipes out its entire internal national debt. This hardly requires explanation, because it is obvious that a bond of a thousand marks is wiped out when the mark is worth nothing. The government has practiced the rankest kind of thievery upon all those of its citizens who had purchased its obligations (such as the entire War Loans). This does not apply, however, to debts which the government may have owed in other currencies than its own. In the case of Germany there was no foreign debt (debt in foreign money), but there were Reparations to pay in gold or goods or foreign money.

Not only was the national government of Germany free of debt, other than Reparations, but so were most of the states, cities, and big corporations. Their debts, too, had been wiped out.

On the other hand, the only way Germany could pay the annual cash sums required of her as Reparations was by exporting much more than she imported—which was impossible, because other nations would not buy enough German goods. Now, instead of facing the issue then and there, this is what Germany and the Allies did.

Germany said: "I cannot pay."

The Allies said: "Oh, yes, you can, and if you don't, we'll march in."

The Allies were wrong. Germany really could not pay what was demanded. But Germany was even more wrong.

Instead of saying: "We can't, and that's that," she knuckled under and signed first the Dawes Plan and then the Young Plan, knowing perfectly well that she would carry out neither. But Germany had learned something— or thought she had.

She had learned that bankers in other countries, chiefly in England, America, and Holland, were not only willing but anxious to sell the bonds of German enterprises to the investing public in their respective countries. All the Germans found they had to do was to pay a little more interest on their bonds than English, Dutch and American borrowers paid, and a little more commission to the bankers!

For five years Germany sold so many bonds in this way, and got so many credits from foreign bankers to finance her turnover, that she was able to re-equip most of her industry, waste quite a little money on corrupt government, and still meet her Reparations payments!

Do you see what happened? For five years an otherwise adverse balance of payments was made favorable, because the proceeds of the foreign loans were great enough to offset the Reparations payments. And then the crash came.

A bank failed in Austria (the Credit Anstalt). Overnight people began to wonder whether their Central European credits and bonds were safe. The staggering amount of the figures (over two billion dollars of American money in Germany alone) was for the first time realized, and a "run" started on Germany. No one would give credit; everyone thought only of getting out safely; and in the scramble to get out, the bankers pulled the German house down about their own ears and about the ears of the investing public.

Within a few weeks the job was done. Germany, Austria, and Hungary each declared that they had no more foreign funds available with which to make repayments. They passed laws to prohibit their nationals from exporting capital or buying foreign money. Various "freezing agreements" (standstill agreements) were signed, and all the money that had been loaned to these countries was politely informed that it would have to stay there a long time.

That is what happens when there is no intelligent control of bankers in their foreign lending operations. It has nothing to do with the gold standard, but it wrecked the gold standard. It would wreck any international monetary system.

CHAPTER XI

Managed Currency

The post-war processes briefly indicated in the preceding chapter took place not only in Europe and North America, but in South America, Australia, Africa, and the Far East as well; and these processes of economic and financial deterioration led almost everywhere to the perfectly natural philosophy of national, as opposed to international, thinking.

Each country thought of its own trade balance, its own budget troubles, and the protection of its own currency. Each country took measures to insure its own safety, forgetting that such measures could and would be rendered useless by identical action in other countries. No one seemed to realize that the only real and lasting safeguards were those that could be obtained by mutual agreement.

Whether one likes it or not, whether one is a so-called "internationalist" or an "isolationist," the fact remains that all the measures of economic nationalism so far devised break down upon the same difficulty. If you raise your tariff against my goods, it will only give you an advantage until I do the same. If you attempt to push your exports by depreciating your currency—which makes your goods cheaper in my money—the same method is open to me.

And if we both depreciate our currencies, neither of us has an advantage over the other, but both of us have hurt ourselves by cheapening the value of our goods on the world markets.

When, after the War, the Central European currencies first began to depreciate, two things happened:

1. These countries gained a temporary export advantage, which, however, was soon offset by disruption at home and retaliatory measures abroad.

2. The whole financial world, which had taken the gold-standard mechanism for granted, received a rude shock. If one currency would depreciate, people began to wonder whether other currencies would not do the same thing. As a result a terrific speculation in foreign exchange set in all over the world.

A French merchant at Rouen became afraid of the franc and transferred all his money to England. An Italian became afraid of the lira and bought dollars instead. A Japanese sold his yen and bought Dutch florins—and so on throughout the world. This speculation, arising for the most part through fear of loss rather than hope of gain, caused a vast quantity of money to rush back and forth between countries, fleeing always from the weak to the strong. It was this added strain upon the mechanism of international payments that broke the back of the gold standard.

In 1931 England, which had been the chief European sanctuary for frightened money, got into budget difficulties. The pound had been restored to its old gold parity before the necessary adjustments of costs and prices had been made. A radical Labor government had yielded too far in spending money to take care of unemployment. Taxes were high and it seemed impossible, from a political point of view, to raise them further. It seemed equally impossible to reduce expenditures. As these facts became evident, those who had fled for safety to the pound sterling began to be frightened; pounds were sold and dollars bought instead; and a flow of gold started from London to France and America.

Meantime England had not been a wise banker. She had invested a large part of the frightened money temporarily lodged with her banks in loans to Germany, which now turned out to be uncollectible. Therefore she could not call in funds from abroad to meet the sudden drain upon her gold. Accordingly she borrowed $325,000,000 in Paris and $325,000,000 in New York, hoping thereby to stem the tide. As it turned out, these loans only served to advertise the weakness of the British position and hence to accelerate the withdrawals from London. Pretty soon England came to the end of her resources, and in September 1931 she "suspended gold payments."

The pound sterling from that moment became irredeemable paper, detached from gold, and therefore measurable only in terms of its price in other currencies. An "equalization fund" was set up to regulate this price—not to depress it, but to keep it from fluctuating too widely—and in this way the pound became a "managed currency." It is important to realize that all this was not done because the

British wanted to abandon gold and adopt something which they thought would be better, but because they could not help themselves.

Almost immediately a number of other countries, notably the British Dominions and Scandinavia, followed suit. Their trade was so closely tied up with the British currency that for them any other course was likewise impossible.

And now we come to the curious part of the story, which has led so many people to the wrong conclusion.

The pound, and the other currencies that had gone off gold with it, dropped to about eighty per cent of the gold parity, and almost instantly conditions in the "off-gold countries" began to improve.

In part this was due to the export advantage they obtained over the countries whose currencies, like ours, were still at par. In part it was due to the fact that things always improve when an event that everyone has been afraid of has actually taken place. But, most important of all, things in England began to improve because a new national government came in, cleaned house, put the budget in order, and proceeded to reduce government expenditures.

As this went on, other countries, such as Japan and the South American republics, followed the British example. All these countries went off gold and adopted "managed currencies." The thing that very few people realized was that the "management" of these currencies was only possible because a few other countries—France, Holland, Switzerland, and the United States—remained "on gold."

The method by which the equalization fund "managed"

the pound was very simple. If the pound was too strong, the fund bought francs or dollars. If the pound was too weak, the fund sold these foreign currencies.

There was no great risk in this business, because the fund dealt only in currencies which were convertible into gold. In other words, if the fund bought dollars in large amounts, it would convert these dollars into gold at the Federal Reserve Bank and take the gold home. (Sometimes it would leave the gold on deposit, under what was called an "earmark," which meant that the actual gold—not paper dollars—belonged to the fund.) The same thing was done by the fund in Paris, in Amsterdam, and in Zurich. In plain words, we, the gold countries, were the very convenient bar upon which the off-gold countries pulled themselves up or down as they liked. They could "manage" so long as someone else held the gold bar for them.

And the important thing to realize, to which we shall revert when we come to analyze our own actions in the past year, is that *the management of the off-gold managed currencies was done by means of gold*—via the currencies that were still on a gold standard.

We shall see in Part II, when we come to the Warren Era, how, while talking about gold as an outworn fetish, we ourselves could devise no other means than gold to accomplish what we conceived to be our purpose.

CHAPTER XII

The Commodity Dollar

In a previous chapter, "Money and Prices," we have examined in bare outline the basic elements of the "quantity theory" of money. We have seen that increasing the circulating supply of money often means to decrease its value in terms of things—that is, to raise prices. Also we have noted that the supply of money is not the actual amount in existence, but rather the amount that circulates, so that increasing the rapidity of circulation has the same effect as increasing the amount of money in circulation.

Proceeding from this theory, certain economists go so far as to say that money must not be based upon gold, because then the amount of money is limited by the amount of gold in existence, and that means that we are in constant danger of not having enough money. If there is too little money, money becomes expensive, which is the same thing as saying that prices go down. Then they reason backwards and say that if prices have gone down, it must be because there is too little money; and if there is too little money, it must be because there is too little gold. That is why they want to get away from gold and adopt what is variously called an "index dollar," a "compensated dollar," or a "commodity dollar."

Before we examine what this proposal means, let us have a look at the reasoning behind it.

"If prices have gone down, it must be because there is too little money." In regard to this statement we must observe:

1. That prices may have gone down because of too little money, but also they may have gone down because of too many things. We know, for instance, that wheat has gone down because there has been more grown in the world in proportion to the amount required, and that it is grown in more countries than it used to be. Probably prices have gone down, not because there is too little money, but because there were too many of some things produced, or because of a combination of both.

2. When we say "too little money," we know now that we mean "too little money circulating."

That may be because there is actually not enough money in existence, or because the money that there is does not move around. Consequently, increasing the supply of currency will not raise prices, unless the additional supply gets into circulation.

If we look at the figures in this country, we see that in 1926, when prices were very high, there was actually less currency outstanding than in 1932, when prices were very low. It would seem, therefore, that the reason prices fell so violently was not because there was not enough money in existence, but because money circulated more and more slowly.

3. If what we have just said is correct, then the fact that

the amount of gold in the world might limit the amount of money to a sum too small to maintain decent prices seems rather remote. But, as a matter of fact, even this remote possibility is by no means a certainty. From time to time there have always been new discoveries of gold, and there is no reason to suppose that the world's output of gold necessarily must fall behind the world's production of other things. If it keeps pace, as it has in the past, there is nothing in the whole argument.

As to the various proposals for a non-gold currency, what they amount to is this:

Instead of having a dollar of fixed gold content—which means that a dollar shall be a warehouse receipt for so many grains of gold—it is proposed to have a dollar of varying gold content, but of fixed purchasing power. In other words, people are to be given the assurance that prices of things will not change, in place of the assurance that the price of gold will not change.

If this were feasible, it would undoubtedly make life less complicated. But it is not feasible. To keep the price of gold fixed in terms of money—which is what the gold standard does—is a comparatively simple thing. Gold is a single commodity, a commodity of limited though increasing amount, and it is difficult to obtain.

"Things," on the other hand, include thousands of different kinds of articles, some important, some of no importance. "Things," moreover, include services, such as brain-work and spade-work, the work of a teacher and the labor of a stevedore. "Things" also are subject to sudden unpredictable happenings, such as droughts, storms, and earthquakes—not to mention wars. Under these circumstances it is easy to say that the prices of "things" in terms of money shall be constant, but not so easy to accomplish it.

To meet this difficulty, the advocates of the theory use a price index. They admit that they cannot stabilize each "thing" in terms of money, but they say: "We can stabilize the composite price of all things."

So they make up their index, which is nothing but a combination of what they consider the important prices, and then propose to keep this index figure constant in terms of money. And it is interesting to note that the way they propose to keep this index constant is by increasing or decreasing the amount of gold in the dollar.

We need not concern ourselves here with the theoretical side of this proposal. We need only ask ourselves a few practical questions:

1. Who is going to be wise enough to decide what prices should be used in making up the index?

2. Who is going to be wise enough to know how to "weight" these prices? (If wheat is twice as important as sugar, then the price of wheat, in a weighted index, will be figured twice in compiling the average, while sugar is figured once.) Who is to know the relative importance of potatoes and woollen underwear?

3. Who is to decide how often, or under what circumstances, the index is to be changed? (A few years ago, for instance, there was no artificial silk.)

4. Are seasonal fluctuations, such as occur in the prices of

fruits, to be compensated for by changing the gold price? Who decides that?

5. And, if human intelligence was inadequate to cope with the comparatively simple mechanism of the gold standard, why should we blandly assume that this same human intelligence will be able to work the exceedingly delicate and complicated machinery necessary to keep thousands of prices in adjustment?

6. If governments have shown themselves weak in the past whenever political considerations have been at loggerheads with sound economics, why should we give them a money mechanism which is infinitely more susceptible of political skullduggery than the gold standard?

These are all purely practical objections, to which I for one have never been given any practical answers. And until there are satisfactory answers, it seems to me that the whole idea is one which belongs in the laboratory rather than in the realm of everyday life.

And even if these questions could be answered, how on earth will index money prove satisfactory unless other nations likewise adopt it? How are international balances to be settled, except by shipping gold? And, when you consider that in each nation there is at least one professor who has invented "the perfect money," that no two of these professors agree with each other, and that it is most unlikely that all the nations will ever agree to select one of them as the money messiah, is it not evident that the less you worry about the whole thing, the better?

CHAPTER XIII

A Modernized Gold Standard

Although I have characterized the compensated index dollar as a theoretical dream rather than as a proposal of practical merit, it must not be assumed that I believe that there should be no change in the international gold standard as we knew it before the War. There is much that can be learned from recent experience, and it would be nothing less than criminal if we failed to make certain improvements over the system of the past.

What improvements should be considered is a rather technical matter, which I hesitate to include here. In a nutshell, they consist of two things:

1. We must protect ourselves against the hoarding of gold and against speculative movements of metal. To a large extent this can be done by adopting a "gold bullion standard" (instead of coin), and by understanding and careful control of foreign lending operations between countries.

2. We must be more economical in the use of gold as a monetary metal. There are various ways in which this can be done.

For such readers as may be interested, I have included in the appendix two open letters which I addressed to Senator

Borah on November 28 and December 7, 1933, in which I have gone into the matter quite fully. The ideas suggested are not my own. They are a distillation of the ideas of many others, gathered from months of study and conversation in Washington and at the London Conference. Had the Monetary Conference been able to continue its labors without interruption, I feel quite certain that it would have developed in detail a modernized gold standard, suitable to present-day conditions.

It would not have developed—and no future conference will develop—a monetary system which would automatically prevent booms and depressions, or cure any existing maldistribution of wealth. There will be depressions so long as we do not learn to check booms. There will be maldistribution of wealth until we change our basic conception of the relation of the individual to the community. That cannot be done by adopting a new money mechanism.

CHAPTER XIV

The Stormy Sea of Silver

And now, before we proceed to brief consideration of what we have done in money matters during the past twelve months, let us venture for a moment upon the stormy sea of silver.

What I shall say will probably please no one, because, for some strange reason, you have to be either an ardent bimetallist (or symmetalist) or else one of those who sees red whenever anyone so much as mentions silver. It seems to me there are several aspects to the question.

Silver is an older monetary metal than gold. That does not mean that it is better adapted to use as money. In fact, even the most ardent theoretical silver advocates would, I suppose, agree that if there were a lot more gold than there is in the world, they would not bother so much about silver. The reason gold is a better money metal is that its production does not usually involve producing anything else, whereas silver is largely a by-product of other metals, such as copper and lead. Therefore the amount of silver produced varies more from year to year, because if people want more copper and lead, they have to produce more silver. Since the amount produced varies more, so does the price vary, and therefore it is a less stable base for money than gold.

The whole question boils down to whether there is enough gold in the world to act as a base for the money we require. If there is enough gold, there is to my mind no silver question. If we economize in the use of gold, as suggested in the previous chapter, I do not believe that there is any danger of gold scarcity.

At one time we had silver and gold used side by side, with a ratio fixed by law. It was decreed that fifteen or sixteen ounces of silver should be the equivalent of one ounce of gold. That is bimetallism. Fifteen or sixteen to one was selected because there was about fifteen times as much silver produced as gold. The trouble with bimetallism is that, because silver production varies, people have never considered silver quite so trustworthy as gold. As a result, wherever they have existed side by side, gold, being more popular, has been hoarded and has disappeared from circulation.

Moreover, if there is over-production of silver, a silver-producing country could flood a bimetallic country with silver and draw out all that country's gold. If we had free coinage of silver, for instance (which is the same thing as bimetallism), Mexico could produce a lot of cheap silver, send it to the U. S. Mint to be coined, exchange the silver coins for gold at 16 to 1, and take home the gold. Pretty soon Mexico would be on gold and we should be on silver.

Symmetalism has an advantage over bimetallism, in that under this system you make an alloy of the two metals (some would use even more than two), and that prevents silver draining out the gold. This drainage business, by the way, is what is called "Gresham's Law"—a law which is usually summarized as "Bad money will always drive out good money." Symmetalism will only work, however, if all countries adopt it, because no country could afford to melt up its gold and mix it with other metals unless it knew it could settle international balances of payment in such an alloy. *If* all the nations should ever become convinced that there is really not enough gold in the world, international agreement for symmetalism is not improbable.

That is really all there is to the silver question, although a great deal more is attributed to it. There is, for instance, the argument—an old favorite—that we must raise the price of silver to increase the purchasing power of the Chinaman. The Chinaman uses silver as money. Therefore, it is claimed, if silver were worth more, the Chinaman could buy more of our goods, and that would be good for us and for him. To see what nonsense this is, you have only to realize that the people who argue this way are the very same people who want our dollar made cheaper, because that would make us happier. If it is good for us to depreciate our currency, why should it be good for the Chinaman to increase the value of his currency?

There is also the old chestnut that in 1873 "silver was demonetized in the United States by stealth." Bryan used that one years before the Reverend Charles E. Coughlin exhumed it again. And Theodore Roosevelt answered Bryan in a speech before the American Republican College

League in Chicago, on October 15, 1896, as follows:

" . . . Many of the arguments of our foes are difficult to meet, simply because they are so absurd that it is hard to speak patiently about them. One of these is the talk about what the lunatic portion of our opponents are fond of calling 'the crime of 1873' when, as they say, silver was 'demonetized by stealth.' As a matter of fact the bill which demonetized silver was before the two Houses of Congress for over two years: it was printed thirteen different times and the proceedings in relation to it occupied nearly 150 pages of the Congressional Record. It was passed by large votes after full debate, during which very able speeches in its behalf were made, among others by Senator Jones and Stewart of Nevada who are now among the least rational of the friends of silver. It was scattered broadcast throughout the country and opinions as to its value obtained from every expert in the land; and if its passage was 'stealthy,' then every law that was ever enacted by Congress, from the alien and sedition acts in Adams' administration to the Wilson-Gorman tariff of Cleveland's administration, was passed by 'stealth.' As for its being a crime, you might just as rationally speak of the 'crime' of the demonetization of iron in Sparta about 300 B.C. or the demonetization of cattle in Italy about 1000 B.C."

Most people who want silver money, whether they realize it or not, want cheaper money. If that is the case, they might as well clamor for iron money or tin money or just plain paper money. There is no particular reason they should stop at silver.

On the other hand, silver is used as a medium of exchange by a large part of the world's population—probably by about half—not four fifths, as claimed by the silver-tongued orators. Therefore it is important that silver should fluctuate as little as possible, just as it is desirable that the dollar or the pound fluctuate as little as possible. Otherwise trade between the silver countries of the East and the gold countries becomes difficult and risky.

It is for this reason desirable that steps be taken by international agreement to prevent excessive dumping of silver on the world market, and it is for this reason also that I believe it would be profitable to study the steps I have suggested in my letter to Senator Borah. (See Appendix, pages 255 and 256.)

PART TWO

A YEAR OF ROOSEVELT

CHAPTER XV

What Roosevelt Inherited

It is a curious and perhaps fortunate characteristic of human nature that we forget a painful experience and remember a pleasant one. At the same time that we thus tend to see the past through somewhat rosy spectacles, we are inclined to view the present with the opposite emphasis, exaggerating our woes a little and failing to appreciate fully the pleasant things that happen to us, until long after they have occurred. And so it is that in the worry of today many of us have probably already forgotten the state of utter collapse in which we found ourselves a year ago, when Franklin D. Roosevelt entered upon the scene.

No American President ever took over a nastier, stickier, more complicated mess than did F. D. Roosevelt in March 1933.

Between twelve and fifteen million workers were unemployed; they and their families were literally face to face with starvation. Think what that alone means—nearly a third of our population rapidly approaching the point where the sheer necessity for food and shelter would drive them to any desperate action.

Industry and commerce were practically at a standstill. The farmers were getting less for their crops than it cost to raise them. The entire banking structure had collapsed. Security values had shrunk to microscopic proportions. Foreign debts were uncollectible, and domestic debts had become a staggering burden.

Worst of all, people were discouraged and had lost confidence in their leaders; and the leaders, both business and political, had lost confidence in themselves. Fear walked openly through the land. Anything might have happened.

Probably we came nearer to disaster than we shall ever know.

Before we begin a brief survey of the past twelve months, let us fix in our minds a few of the major problems that confronted the President when he first took office.

1. Unemployment, which threatened social disorder, and called for immediate relief as well as industrial recovery.

2. A Budget problem—that is, how to safeguard the national credit and yet use it to the utmost in bringing about relief and recovery.

3. A collapsed money structure, which had driven gold and currency into hoarding and had tied up billions of dollars of "bank money." This required immediate "unfreezing," as well as measures of reconstruction and reform.

4. An agricultural problem, which demanded immediate relief and permanently higher prices for farm products, in relation to the general price level.

5. An industrial deadlock, which had to be solved in

order to provide permanent re-employment and also in order to restore the values of securities.

6. A railroad dilemma, important for the same reasons as the industrial problem.

7. An international tangle of tariffs, treaties, debts, and currencies, which threatened the destruction of all world trade and which seemed to have brought all nations to the cross-roads of chaos or recovery.

There were many other problems as well, but these seem to me to be the most important.

Viewed from a different aspect, the picture as a whole divided itself into only three major categories: first, problems of immediate relief; second, methods of bringing about recovery, so that continued relief would be unnecessary; and, third, measures of reform, designed to prevent a recurrence of the malady.

To these should be added a fourth problem—namely, how to throw the maximum strength of Government help behind the forces of relief and recovery without impairing the national credit and without imposing on future generations too heavy a burden of taxation.

It is not the purpose of this book, nor am I qualified, to discuss all the aspects of the first year of Roosevelt rule. My purpose is primarily to help clear up some of the issues involved in the "money muddle."

The specific problems of industry and agriculture, for example, lie beyond our sphere; where we touch upon them, it is only because of their being so closely interwoven with money, banking, and finance. What I shall attempt to do is to take note of the various steps that were taken in the general field of money, and to trace through these steps the gradual development of the President's policy.

The steps taken in the general field of money relate to three major topics: the national credit; the national currency; and the banking and investment system.

For the sake of convenience I have listed the most important actions taken with regard to each of these topics. Some of these actions were of an emergency nature; some were not. Irrespective of their original purpose, they combine to give us the sum total of our present policy. Some of the items appear in more than one column, because some of the actions affected more than one of the three major topics.

Currency	*National Credit*	*Banking*
Gold Embargo	Economy Act	Emergency Banking Act
Abandonment of Gold Standard	Abrogation of Gold Clause	Securities Act
Abrogation of Gold Clause	N.R.A.—Public Works	Glass-Steagall Bill
Thomas Amendment	R.F.C. Operations	(Banking Act of 1933)
Instructions to American Delegation Conference	C.W.A.	R.F.C. Operations
July 3rd Message to Conference	Budget Message	Temporary Guarantee Plan
Radio Speech of October 22	Gold Reserve Act	Gold Reserve Act
Gold-Buying Program		Securities Exchange Bill
Silver Proclamation		
Gold Reserve Act		
Devaluation Proclamation		

CHAPTER XVI

March Madhouse

While it is impossible to be sure, it seems reasonably certain that the bottom of the world depression had actually been reached at some time between July and the latter part of 1932. There were signs of recovery in many countries, and it is likely that there would have been such signs here as well if it had not been for the collapse of our banking and currency machinery.

This collapse had its origin in the stock-market boom that ended with the crash of 1929. During the five-year period preceding the 1929 crash our banks had been steadily investing more and more of their funds in securities and loans on securities, and less and less of their funds in commercial "turnover" loans.

As a result "bank money" was outstanding largely against transactions of a capital nature, which, as we have seen, should be taken care of by the investment market. This happened because the whole country was seized by what can only be described as a speculative mania and because the bankers and the Government were not wise enough nor brave enough to put a stop to it in time.

Merchants bought stocks when they should have kept their money working in their own business. Industrial corporations bought stocks of other corporations. Widows sold their bonds and bought stocks. The elevator boy bought stocks—so did the bootblack, the dentist, and the college professor. All they had to do was to pay in a small proportion in cash—the broker loaned them the rest—and wait for the boom to make them rich.

The brokers in turn went to the banks to be carried, and the banks, when they had loaned all their available funds, went to the Federal Reserve Banks to rediscount their commercial bills and lend out the proceeds in still more broker's loans.

Stocks went higher and higher, because everyone was scrambling to get aboard the get-rich-quick wagon, and those who had profits refused to sell out and take them because that would mean paying taxes.

A very few people saw what was coming and warned against it. My father, Paul M. Warburg, was one of them. In March 1929 he issued a public warning against the speculation that was taking place in the security markets. But his voice, and the voices of a few others, were unheard amidst the clamor of the tipsters, the pool operators, and the resonant boomings of the "new era economists." "A good stock should sell for at least twenty times its earnings. It's cheap at anything less"—that was one of the favorite phrases. Professor Irving Fisher, recently again in the limelight through the reflected glory of his disciple Professor Warren, made a number of oracular pronouncements in September and October 1929.

According to the New York *Times* of September 5, 1929,

following Roger Babson's announcement that a stock-market crash was coming, Professor Fisher issued the following statement: "Stock prices are not too high and Wall Street will not experience anything in the nature of a crash." On October 15 Fisher declared in a public address that stock prices had reached "what looks like a permanently high plateau." On October 21 he said that even in the then high market the prices of stocks had not yet caught up with their real values. He explained that the market was not inflated, but only had been readjusted to the decreasing value of the dollar and the increasing pace of production and trade. He said: "In my opinion current predictions of heavy reactions affecting the general level of securities find little if any foundation in fact." On October 23 he said: "Fears that the price level of stocks might go down to where it was in 1923 or earlier, engendered by recent breaks in the market value of securities, are not justified by present economic conditions."

And people believed it—for no other reason than that they wanted to believe it.

When the inevitable crash came, only a week or so later, it is not difficult to see what had to happen. The whole inflated structure had to tumble down. Customers of brokers could no longer put up their margins and were sold out. Brokers went "broke" because they could not sell fast enough. Banks suffered heavy losses not only on their own holdings of securities (which were too large), but through the insolvency of many of their customers. And still the market went down.

After a time people began to realize that this was more than just a "technical set-back"—another favorite "new era" phrase. In the sober light of a new dawn they looked at their battered financial position and realized—most of them—that they had been on a gigantic financial drunk. They realized also the part that bankers had played, or failed to play, in this debauch, and began to wonder whether, after all, bankers were as wise as they were supposed to be.

When people begin to wonder about bankers, it is only a short step before they begin to distrust, and when they distrust, they draw out their money.

That is exactly what happened. At first it was a slow seepage of withdrawal. Here and there a man or woman would go to the bank and draw out currency. Then they told their friends, and their friends went. By and by it became known that such and such a bank was suffering heavy withdrawals. Then there was a run, with queues forming out in the street. Meantime the bank was frantically calling loans, selling out collateral, borrowing where it could borrow—anything to get cash.

Eventually the cash gave out and the bank closed its doors. More often the bank was closed without all this happening, because the bank examiner, seeing that the bank did not have enough liquid assets to meet the probable demand, would close it in the hope of thus saving more for the depositors and of seeing that all got equal treatment.

Bank failures or closings increased steadily throughout 1930, 1931, and 1932. Finally, early in 1933, so many banks got into trouble in Michigan that the Governor declared a "moratorium"—which is a polite word for closing all the banks. That was the signal for the real panic to begin.

So far, with a few isolated exceptions, the bank failures had been confined to the smaller banks—most of them in the smaller communities. But when all the big banks in Michigan were closed, it was like pouring gasoline on a slowly smoldering fire.

By the first of March nine out of forty-eight states had closed their banks or issued orders to permit only restricted withdrawals. By the night of March 3 similar action was being taken in every state in the Union.

In their mad rush to get out of the banks the people of the United States took out more than two billion dollars of currency—over $700,000,000 of it in the last week!

They had taken it out of the banks so fast that at the end the Federal Reserve Banks were unable to supply the banks with currency—it could not be printed fast enough!

During this same time the people of the United States had taken out $563,000,000 of gold—more than seventeen per cent of what there was in the vaults of the Federal Reserve Banks when the rush began!

That was what Roosevelt faced when he took the oath of office on March 4, 1933. And right here let me express a conviction, with which many people will perhaps disagree:

I believe that we need never have gone through the ultimate writhings of the panic, as expressed in the closing of all the banks—I believe that we need never have written so disgraceful a page in our financial history—if our day for inaugurating a new President had happened to be January 1 instead of March 4.

I believe that if that same quiet, reassuring voice could have spoken over the radio only a month earlier and calmed the fears of the people as it calmed them in the first week of March, the monetary history of this country—and of the world—would have been vastly different. But that, after all, is only conjecture. We are here concerned with actual events.

Several things happened in this March madhouse that were of vital importance.

In the first place, Mr. Roosevelt won the confidence of the country with his Inaugural Address. From that moment people felt that they had a leader, and fear was on the wane.

In the second place, the President took quick and, on the whole, effective action to unlock the frozen banking structure. First he declared a national moratorium, thus taking the matter out of the hands of the states. Then he set to work a group of financial experts under his Secretary of the Treasury, William Woodin, with instructions to work out a plan that would reopen the sound banks within a week. Then he took the first of a series of steps which resulted in ultimately nationalizing the gold supply, although I doubt if anything more than the immediate necessity of the moment was in his mind at the time.

The first step in nationalizing gold was the order prohibiting any bank from paying out gold without special permission. This was dictated by necessity, because distrust of the currency had gone so far that the minute the banks would be allowed to reopen, people would again begin to withdraw gold.

From this first step followed the second—namely, an embargo (prohibition) on shipments of gold out of the country. This was a necessity of a political nature, because the people would not understand if they were not allowed to obtain gold while a foreigner still could get it.

It was also wise from the point of view of international strategy, because at one stroke it released the United States dollar from being the instrument by which England and the other off-gold countries were managing their currencies. Furthermore, it served notice on Great Britain that two could play the game of managed currency, and was welcomed by those of us who were hoping to see England shortly return to a gold basis.

On the other hand, had Mr. Roosevelt come in a month sooner, or had he seen his way clear to make a strong statement as to his currency views a month prior to his taking office, I doubt very much whether any gold embargo would have been necessary—domestic or foreign. Again this is conjecture, but I believe that the threat of a gold embargo would have been more effective in restoring an international gold standard than the actuality. Nevertheless, with things as they were on March 4, there was very little choice.

There was, however, this important element of choice, in which I have always thought that we chose wrong:

We could, at the time we embargoed gold, have stated that it was our purpose to return to a gold standard as soon as the other off-gold countries would do likewise. By so doing we should have prevented a great deal of speculation, and we should have avoided travelling so far down the dangerous road of currency depreciation. Had we done that, we should have had no "Thomas Amendment," and a good deal less of Professor Warren's theory. But I am getting ahead of my story. We are not quite finished with March.

Within a very short time the Emergency Banking Act was sent to Congress and was passed. This act provided the machinery for the gradual reopening of the banks and, together with the President's assurance over the radio that every bank that was reopened could be considered sound, restored the public's confidence in the safety of their deposits.

The President's assurance also had another and far-reaching effect: it meant that, politically at least, the Government had taken upon itself what amounted to a guarantee that the banks would actually be sound.

Some of us, realizing the danger involved, pleaded for a more stringent control over the state authorities in determining whether their non-member institutions (banks not under Federal supervision) were fit to open, but this proved a political impossibility.

It was this decision that made it necessary later to provide for a guarantee of bank deposits—and that is a subject we shall discuss in a subsequent chapter.

Finally, the President sent to Congress, and Congress enacted, the Economy Bill. This measure pared down

Government expenses, which had swollen under the previous Administration, and particularly did it effect substantial savings by reducing veterans' compensation. It was a brave measure, because it was bound to be an unpopular one. It was a wise measure, because it showed the country that the President was deeply conscious of the importance of maintaining the national credit. Its passage was due largely to the energetic efforts of Lewis Douglas, Director of the Budget.

There were other things that happened in March—many of them of great importance—but none that directly concern our story.

By the end of the month the financial panic was over. Out of some 18,000 banks, over 12,000, with ninety per cent of the country's deposits, had been reopened under license. The stock and commodity exchanges were again functioning. Prices were rising. Ninety-day Treasury bills, which just before the inauguration had sold to yield about four and a half per cent, had risen to a point where they yielded only about one half per cent—which tells the story of the ebb and flow of confidence in the Government's credit.

On the other hand, the Government had embarked upon a dangerous course in suspending shipments of gold abroad without declaring its intention of resuming under the proper conditions. As a result speculation had begun to set in. And, furthermore, the Government had done another risky thing in assuming moral responsibility for the solvency of all the reopened banks, over many of which it had no control.

CHAPTER XVII

April Fool, and Around the Maypole

The first consequences of the March gold action were not long in coming. Through the first half of April the dollar remained fairly close to par. Exports of gold were permitted under license, and the world believed that we had no intention of abandoning the gold standard. Nor had those of us who were in daily contact with the President in regard to monetary matters any idea that he was seriously considering such a move.

In the early days of April much time was devoted to the preparation of a program for discussion with the various foreign missions invited to Washington for the purpose of preparing the ground for the Economic Conference.

In laying out our program for these conversations the crucial point time and again had been the question of how to get the off-gold countries to re-establish a workable international monetary standard. It had been generally recognized that Great Britain and the so-called Sterling Bloc of countries would probably be unable, or at least unwilling, to return at once to their old gold parities.

It had been considered whether perhaps some form of temporary stabilization of the pound, the franc, and the dollar should be tried. And there had also been some talk of a general revaluation of all the currencies in terms of gold by international agreement. It was this latter thought which always seemed to me to hold out the greatest promise of re-establishing law and order.

No one, so far as I know, in the Administration circles, unless it was the President himself, had any idea at that time of embarking upon the course which we subsequently followed.

There was in Congress a strong inflationary group—a group, however, which had almost as many plans as it had members. While these Senators and Congressmen could be counted upon to make a certain number of wild speeches, it seemed highly improbable that they would agree upon any definite proposal; and, even if they did, it seemed even more improbable that they could muster sufficient strength to pass a bill over the President's veto.

There were, however, other forces beginning to make themselves felt. A small group of industrialists, later enlarged, had formed themselves into a committee to propagate the idea of devaluing the dollar by reducing its gold content. This group chose for itself the modest title of "The Committee for the Nation."

Apparently amply supplied with funds, this committee proceeded to enlist the services of economists, notably Professor Warren of Cornell, and to circularize all members of Congress, Administration officials, and even such unofficial advisers as myself. They proceeded also to spread very ably conceived propaganda throughout all parts of the country. The directing committee of the "Committee for the Nation" consisted of the following members:

Chairman: J. H. Rand, Jr., President, of Remington
Rand, Inc.

F. H. Frazier, Chairman, General Baking
Co.

Lessing J. Rosenwald, Chairman, Sears, Roe-
buck & Co.

F. H. Sexauer, President, Dairymen's League
Co-op. Assn., Inc.

Among its supporting members there were a considerable number of prominent citizens, many of whom, I discovered later, knew very little about what they were supporting. Some of them, prominent in the committee's early
activities, later chose to dissociate themselves from its propaganda.

An important though unseen figure in this organization
is a Dr. E. A. Rumely, whose colorful past history includes
a conviction under the Trading with the Enemy Act.

While the Committee for the Nation was moving in
industrial and business circles, Senator Thomas, the dap-
per, white-haired Oklahoman, was skillfully organizing in
Congress the various inflationary groups of the South,
West, and Middle West, deriving much of his intellectual
ammunition from George LeBlanc, the former head of the
foreign department of one of the large Wall Street banks.
So far as I know, LeBlanc was one of the earliest advocates
of our abandoning the gold standard and devaluing the

dollar. His influence also made itself felt upon the Reverend Charles E. Coughlin, whose fiery sermons from the Shrine of the Little Flower in Detroit served to fan the flame of inflation among the masses.

Thus, when one analyzes the original forces for inflation —or devaluation, or greenbacks, or silver—one sees a curiously small and compact picture: Rumely and his group of industrialists, Thomas and his group of supporters in the Senate and the House, Father Coughlin and his ever-increasing millions of radio listeners, and LeBlanc with his knowledge of the workings of exchange acquired from years of international finance.

To return to our story—the dollar held fairly close to par during the early part of April, because no one seriously believed that we would permanently cut loose from gold. As the inflationists in Congress began to mutter and rumble, however, the question began to be asked what stand the President would take.

So far he had carefully avoided defining his attitude. The rumblings increased to a roar, notably from Senator Thomas of Oklahoma, and still the White House preserved a serene silence. By the middle of the month the dollar had gone to a five per cent discount. The "gold export point" was reached.

On the 15th of the month several banks applied for licenses to export gold. The licenses were granted, and the world heaved a sigh of relief as the dollar regained its strength. But this illusion was short-lived. Three days later the President announced that no more licenses would be issued and that we were now definitely "off the gold standard." Down went the dollar until it reached a discount of about thirteen per cent at the end of the month.

In the meantime the British mission, headed by Prime Minister Ramsay MacDonald, was on the water, and the French were about to set sail. Can you imagine their bewilderment when they received the news? But that was not all—oh, by no means all.

Simultaneously with his decision to abandon the gold standard the President approved the so-called Thomas Amendment to the Farm Relief Act.

This amendment, as originally introduced by Senator Elmer Thomas, gave the President practically unlimited power to inflate the currency by printing greenbacks, or to depreciate the currency by reducing its gold content (devaluation), or to adopt bimetallism, or to "manage" by practically any means he might see fit. Accordingly, Thomas could count upon the support of the greenbackers, the devaluationists, and the silver enthusiasts. It was a measure which confessed clearly that its author did not care by what means inflation and "cheap money" were brought about, so long as they arrived. Greenbacks, silver, and devaluation were all one to Senator Thomas, so long as something happened immediately.

When, on the same night of April 17, the President told a group of his advisers that, while he wanted certain modifications and limitations, he had agreed to this proposal, I can still see the looks on some of the faces.

All argument—and there was plenty of it from a few of

us—proved unavailing. Some of the worst features of the proposal were eliminated or changed, but its general character remained. The President felt that it was better to let Congress pass a "permissive" inflationary bill than to run the risk of their attempting to pass a "mandatory" one. The Thomas proposal gave the power to the President to do various things, but did not make it compulsory for him to do them—another bill might leave him no choice.

One of the reasons given for the Administration's fear of a mandatory bill was the fact that Senator Wheeler's 16-to-1 silver bill had a few days previously received thirty-three votes in the Senate. This vote was, however, entirely misleading. Many Senators voted for the bill only because they felt sure that it had no chance to pass.

Personally I have never believed that Congress would have passed any measure at that time over the veto, or even against the expressed desire, of the President.

The effect of White House approval of this measure was instantaneous. The dollar dropped; stocks and commodities rose; the Committee for the Nation and all the various inflationary groups acclaimed their victory, while those, here and abroad, who had had some experience of what inflation would do to a country, stood aghast.

The British mission arrived, followed shortly by the French, the Italians, and others—from Europe, Asia, and North and South America. With all these nations plans were discussed for the rapidly approaching World Conference. To all these nations we said that one of the primary purposes of the Conference must be the re-establishment

lieving that maintenance of existing gold parities is in the interest of world recovery.

"Governments subscribing to this declaration whose currencies are not on the gold standard take note of the above declaration and recognize its importance without in any way prejudicing their own future ratios to gold, and reiterate that the ultimate objective of their currency policy is to bring back an international standard based on gold under proper conditions.

"Each government whose currency is not on the gold standard agrees to adopt such measures as it may deem most effective to limit exchange speculations, and other signatory governments undertake co-operation to the same end.

"Each of the governments signatory hereto agrees to ask its central bank to work together with the central banks of other governments which sign this declaration in limiting speculation and, at the proper time, reinaugurating an international gold standard."

Once more the totally unexpected happened. Not only did the President refuse to approve of the declaration, but he sent a message to the Conference that made its death only a matter of days. This message was of such importance that I quote it in full:

President Roosevelt's Statement

I would regard it as a catastrophe amounting to a world tragedy if the great conference of nations, called to bring about a more real and permanent financial stability and a greater prosperity to the masses of all nations, should, in advance of any serious effort to consider these broader problems, allow itself to be diverted by the proposal of a purely artificial and temporary experiment affecting the monetary exchange of a few nations only.

"Such action, such diversion, shows a singular lack of proportion and a failure to remember the larger purposes for which the economic conference originally was called together.

"I do not relish the thought that insistence on such action should be made an excuse for continuance of the basic economic errors that underlie so much of the present worldwide depression.

"The world will not long be lulled by the specious fallacy of achieving a temporary and probably an artificial stability in foreign exchange on the part of a few large countries only.

"The sound internal economic system of a nation is a greater factor in its well-being than the price of its currency in changing terms of the currencies of other nations.

"It is for this reason that reduced costs of government, adequate government income, and ability to service its government debts are all so important to ultimate stability.

"So, too, old fetishes of so-called international bankers are being replaced by efforts to plan national currencies with the objective of giving to those currencies a continuing purchasing power which does not greatly vary in terms of the commodities and need of modern civilization.

"Let me be frank in saying that the United States seeks

the kind of dollar which a generation hence will have the same purchasing power and debt-paying power as the dollar value we hope to attain in the near future. That objective means more to the good of other nations than a fixed ratio for a month or two in terms of the pound or franc.

"Our broad purpose is permanent stabilization of every nation's currency. Gold or gold and silver can well continue to be a metallic reserve behind currencies, but this is not the time to dissipate gold reserves. When the world works out concerted policies in the majority of nations to produce balanced budgets and living within their means, then we can properly discuss a better distribution of the world's gold and silver supply to act as a reserve base of national currencies.

"Restoration of world trade is an important partner both in the means and in the result. Here also temporary exchange fixing is not the true answer. We must rather mitigate existing embargoes to make easier the exchange of products of which one nation has and the other nation has not.

"The conference was called to better and perhaps to cure fundamental economic ills. It must not be diverted from that effort."

It is not difficult to see how the tone of this document shocked the representatives of the nations assembled in London perhaps even more than its content. As long as I live, I shall not forget the expression on Ramsay Mac-Donald's face when Governor Cox and I called upon him with this message, nor shall I forget the expression on the faces of the hundreds of delegates that crowded around the bulletin board at Kensington that day—nor the comments we had to listen to and read in the European press. Some of the comments I have kept verbatim. They would make interesting reading, but it would not be discreet to repeat them now.

One voice was lifted in a pæan of praise: J. Maynard Keynes, the well-known English economist, proclaimed "Roosevelt magnificently right."

Perhaps he was—perhaps the President alone had a vision of a goal that others could not see. To me it seemed a message that could not possibly have come from the man whom I had learned to love and admire, and not the least for his qualities of kindliness and understanding.

The French in particular were incensed. Here are two samples:

Pertinax, in the *Echo de Paris:*

"Mr. Roosevelt goes so far as to denounce the French budgetary deficit. We did not know he was so rigorously correct in matters of public finance. Has not he preached the utmost expenditures by the State in order to raise prices? This trait is revealing. It demonstrates that the President composed his message during a crisis of ill humor."

The *Petit Journal:*

"It is permitted to ask oneself now how the London conference can do an efficacious job in the midst of a general dance of currencies."

From July 3rd on, the conference was as dead as a last

year's popular song. For three weeks it went on twitching, before it finally rolled over and lay still on the 27th. The fact that it did not break up in a state of chaos and anger at President Roosevelt was due to the patient determination of one man, Cordell Hull. The American Secretary of State —his lifelong dream of international economic understanding shattered—his policies thrown into the discard—fought for three weeks for no other purpose than to keep the blame for having wrecked the hopes of the world from falling too heavily upon his President.

For a few days after the receipt of the fatal message the cables were kept humming between the White House and Claridge's Hotel, in a vain effort to understand what the President meant by a dollar of constant purchasing power.

Could it be that he had suddenly become convinced of the commodity dollar theory? How was it possible to reconcile that with our carefully worked out instructions?

Nobody knew, and the cables from Washington only made matters more confusing.

It was our job—mine in particular—to interpret to the other delegations what our new monetary policy signified. Being completely unable to do so, I wrote Mr. Hull:

London, July 6, 1933

Dear Mr. Secretary,

It is clear from the President's messages of the last few days that he now has in mind a monetary and currency program which differs quite radically from that which formed the basis of his original instructions to us. I have carefully studied his cables in an endeavor to find out just what sort of a monetary and currency program he now wants to develop, and I think that I see certain ideas forming in his mind which may well lead to an entirely different and more effective currency system than the world has yet known. The idea of a commodity dollar, or of a currency based partly on commodity prices, is not new but it is a line of thought which has certainly never been developed to its full possibilities. The idea of an international gold unit of exchange is more novel still and also presents an interesting field for further thought and study. Whether or not the two ideas can be reconciled I do not know, but certainly it would be interesting to get the President's ideas in full detail and endeavor to develop fully the new program, the basic elements of which are contained in his recent messages to us.

On the other hand, it seems clear to me that this new thought has not been sufficiently developed at the moment to enable us to proceed here at the Conference to preach the new gospel. It is my personal conviction that it will take us more than a few weeks to work out a currency plan better than anything that the combined brains of the world have been able to develop over a period of centuries, and it is for that reason that I have, as you know, urged that we should not oppose a three months' recess but should welcome it in order that we might go home to attempt to work out such a new program.

The President's repeated instructions on this point were, however, that we must at all costs keep the Conference *alive, and you have by extraordinary skill succeeded in preventing an adjournment which two days ago seemed inevitable. The result of the continuation of the Conference will be that we shall be asked to define clearly what is meant by the new currency program indicated in the President's message. I do not feel that I can interpret his mind at a distance of 3,000 miles, nor do I feel that the new plan is sufficiently crystallized in his mind to enable him to give us complete clarity by cable or telephone or, for that matter, by letter. No matter how good the plan may eventually be, it will in its very nature be an experiment and I do not feel that we can urge such an experiment upon other nations at the present time and under the present circumstances. For these reasons I feel that I must ask you to accept my resignation as financial adviser of the American Delegation, on the very simple ground that we are entering upon waters for which I have no charts and in which I therefore feel myself an utterly incompetent pilot.*

If, after I have returned to the United States, I can be of any help, it is needless to say I shall always be glad to do so. I have written you at such length in order to make my position perfectly clear and avoid any misunderstanding or misconstruction which might be put upon my action at this time.

Very sincerely yours,
JAMES P. WARBURG

The Honorable Cordell Hull,
Secretary of State,
Claridge's, London.

Mr. Hull agreed that the most useful thing I could do would be to return to Washington at once, and accordingly I sailed on the first available steamer. On the way home I prepared several memoranda for the President, one of which, because it is the quickest way of telling the story, I include here.

July 24, 1933

Memorandum on
Domestic Currency Problem

The Administration has, in my judgment, never faced a more serious situation than it does today. The entire recovery program, which is the heart of its policy, is jeopardized by uncertainty and doubt in the monetary field. The National Recovery Act cannot possibly function to any useful end if there is fear of currency depreciation of an unknown amount and fear as to monetary experimentation. There has already been a tremendous flight of capital, and this flight will continue at an increasing pace so long as uncertainty prevails.

Furthermore, while the threat of inflation originally acted as a stimulus to buying of commodities, and therefore as a stimulus to production and trade, it is obvious that the rise of prices and production, stimulated by fear of money, has far outstripped reality and now constitutes a menace in itself.

In the international field, the feeling that we were embarked upon a well-ordered program is rapidly shifting into a feeling that we are fumbling about in the dark, and a continuation of our present undefined monetary policy will inevitably result in further monetary chaos in other countries. The line of probable events is perfectly clear but too long a story to include in this memorandum.

I therefore urgently recommend the following:

1. That all monetary ideas, projects and studies be concentrated in one place, and it would seem to me that the logical place would be the Treasury Department and the Federal Reserve Board.

2. That it be decided now what authorities are to be consulted in preparing a definite monetary program; that a commission be formed of these authorities immediately; and that this commission be given not over a month to prepare a recommendation to the Treasury.

3. That the terms of reference for the commission be defined as follows:

(a) That the United States Government desires not later than October 1st to fix the amount of devaluation which is desired in order to bring about the necessary adjustment of the price level, allowing for a subsequent variation of not over 10%.

(b) That the United States Government desires to enter into conversations as soon as possible with the other countries now off gold with a view to their likewise fixing their ratios to gold with a variation of 10%, at the same time that we fix ours.

(c) Acting on assumptions (a) and (b), the commission is asked to determine two things:

A. What amount of devaluation should be fixed for

the United States dollar. For example, if a seventy cent dollar is the answer, this would mean a definite declaration that devaluation will not exceed 35% or be less than 25%, the actual figure to be determined over a period of time.

B. What should be the exact nature of the gold standard to which the United States returns in the autumn? How can the pre-war gold standard be improved, and how can the purchasing power of the currency be rendered more stable without resorting to methods so academic and so untried that their adoption would in itself again disturb confidence?

I believe it is perfectly possible for the commission to evolve an improved gold standard, and I have a definite idea as to how a gold standard can be made more likely to provide price stability than it did in the past. I believe further that in a program such as is outlined above, we would have the active support not only of Great Britain and the Dominions, but of the Scandinavian countries and eventually even of the gold countries. The result would be that in the autumn the off-gold countries would return to a ratio to gold on an improved gold standard and that the gold countries would very quickly adopt the new standard, some of them possibly taking this opportunity to revalue their currencies overnight without ever getting into the position of running amuck as we are doing at the present moment. If such a program is not adopted, I foresee grave danger not only domestically in the breakdown of our entire program, but internationally, in that by the time we are compelled to stabilize in the interests of our domestic picture, the present gold countries will have gone off gold and will be just where we are today.

J. P. W.

July Jitters

While all this was going on abroad, the Glass-Steagall Bill had become law, when the President signed the Banking Act of 1933 on June 17. This law contains much that is good. It provided at last the much-needed separation of the investment business from the commercial banking business. It stressed the necessity of confining the creation of "bank money" to banks which do not invest their funds in speculative loans, but it was only a first step in the right direction.

Meanwhile the Senate investigation had shown up some of the bad practices indulged in by certain large banks and bankers. Undoubtedly this was a necessary and good thing to do, but it had the unfortunate effect of creating the impression in the minds of many people that, since a few banks had been badly managed, all banks very likely looked the same way. This tendency to lump all bankers as scoundrels—arising from the obvious failure of bankers as a whole to do their job properly, and fostered by inflammatory utterances of demagogues—has made it difficult for honest bankers (and there are many of them) to be as useful in the process of reconstruction as they would like to be.

The most important—and, to my mind, the worst—feature of the Banking Act was the provision for a guarantee of deposits. Under this law a plan is provided which makes all banks mutually responsible. One bank is therefore no better and no worse than any other bank, and no bank knows to what extent it may be called upon to make up the losses of others.

Before leaving for London at the end of May I left a memorandum in Washington, stressing the dangers of this proposal. In it I said:

Memorandum for Raymond Moley

"If the present bill passes and becomes law, any sensible person who has a large investment in a commercial bank or who is engaged in the career of commercial banking will reach the conclusion that the game is not worth the candle. . . .

"If the qualifications for admission into the insurance fund are severe, thousands of banks throughout the country will be unable to qualify and will inevitably fail because people will take their money out of banks that do not belong to the insurance group. If the qualifications for membership, on the other hand, are lax, every decent bank will be forced to consider seriously getting out of the Federal Reserve System so as to avoid participating in the insurance plan. It does not take a long consideration of this question to lead one to the conclusion that one might just as well liquidate as try to run a bank of any size outside of the Federal Reserve System.

"That means that the banking business will fall in the lap of the Government completely.

"The good banks will either become bad banks or go out of business, and the bad banks in the last analysis will belong to the R.F.C."

At that time, before we left for London, it looked as if the guarantee plan would be revised, but in the hurry of the last days of the Congressional session, the bill became law without modification. We shall see the consequences a little later.

While the London Conference was slowly breathing its last, and while I was on the water coming home, the dollar fell lower and lower, and prices rose higher and higher. By July 18 the dollar had dropped to about 69 cents; wheat was $1.24, against 68 cents in April; cotton was just twice its price of February 1—11¾ cents per pound as against less than 6 cents; stocks reached an average price of 98.05, as compared to 46.85 on March 2.

And then the inevitable happened. In three days of near panic wheat dropped to a little over 90 cents, cotton to about 8 cents, and stocks lost over 21 points. The grain exchanges were closed. Stock exchanges shortened their hours. Everything was done to stem the tide of reaction. The very thing to prevent which we had wrecked the London Conference had happened!

Within a few days the storm was over, and prices began slowly to recover.

It was in the midst of this that I returned to Washington. A curious change had taken place in the atmosphere. It was almost as if international problems, the Conference, and all such matters had been forgotten, or even had never existed. On all sides there was talk only of one thing, the N.R.A. and how it would bring about an instant and miraculous recovery. Prices were being scanned anew every hour. People rushed in and out of offices with charts, on which the latest colored inks had not yet dried. Everything that happened was greeted as a proof of how right we were. Codes were being rushed through and signed. General Johnson rode clattering through the streets in full panoply as the people cheered a new national hero. General Johnson made a speech. General Johnson had a cold. The coal industry, the window-cleaners, the railroads, the soda-jerkers, signed up, or refused to sign, or were about to sign. Wheat was up a cent—so was cotton. The dollar was down —so was the thermometer. Johnson! Johnson! N.R.A.! Blue Eagle! Whoopee!

To one coming back after six weeks abroad it seemed as if the whole country had gone raving mad.

After a time, when one's eyes and ears became accustomed to the commotion, one could see that certain things were really being accomplished. Child labor, the sweatshop, the coal industry were being cleaned up. There really was a certain amount of re-employment. There really was an increase in business activity. General Johnson really was doing a heroic job—but—

Under the banner of the Blue Eagle industry was being regimented without sufficient regard to the individual conditions in each enterprise, or even group of enterprises. Sauce for the gander was not only sauce for the goose, but for the soup and fish and strawberry tart as well. Indigestion seemed indicated. And—

Under the wage-raising drive of the General, costs of manufacturing were rising, and sooner or later costs of goods to the consumer would have to rise as well. And—

Under the wing of the Blue Eagle there was hatching a program of government spending—Public Works, and later Civil Works—which would make curious reading alongside of the President's avowed principles concerning a balanced budget.

Worst of all, the uncertainty in regard to our monetary policy—the uncertainty as to what kind of dollar we were going to have, as well as how big or how small a dollar— was keeping more and more business men from making any long-range commitments. The more the doubt grew, the less people were willing to risk making a contract for more than a few weeks ahead, because no one could calculate where or what the dollar would be by October.

This was the sort of thing many of us were saying to the President, urging him every day to remove uncertainty and announce a clearly defined monetary policy. Granted that we could not return immediately to a fixed ratio to gold, it did seem as though there was nothing to lose and much to gain by at least defining the limits within which stabilization would ultimately take place.

The President listened with great patience and understanding—to both sides. On what I would call "the other side" were the adherents of the Warren school, the inflation-

ists of all sorts, and, of course, our old friend, the Committee for the Nation.

All through August and September the battle was waged, with the scene shifting from Washington to Hyde Park, from Hyde Park to New York, where Woodin was recovering from a long illness, back to Hyde Park, and down again to Washington, when the President returned from his brief vacation. It was a battle not so much of men as of two conflicting schools of thought—with the President acting as a tireless, serene, and often amused referee.

In the end it was not conviction that the Warren theory was right so much as the fact that Warren offered a program of action—a program more suited to the immediate political necessities—that carried the day. Warren said—and believed—that he had a quick cure. We admitted that we had none, and we doubted whether there could be any monetary cure for troubles that we believed were not monetary in nature or origin.

CHAPTER XX

Charts and Graphs

Almost the first thing the President said to me when we started to discuss the money problem in late July, immediately after my return from London, was: "I want you to talk to Warren and Rogers." And the first thing I did after leaving the White House was to make an appointment with these two newest prophets of the New Deal.

James Harvey Rogers of Yale I had seen before and knew to be a believer in spending one's way out of trouble without much regard to the Budget. I knew also that he had a firmly imbedded notion that our price level depended more upon the dollar-sterling exchange rate than upon any other factor. In the early days of the Administration he appeared in Washington, where I listened to him at Raymond Moley's request and heard him expound his belief that the essential thing for the Government to do was to spend hundreds of millions per month on grade crossings.

George F. Warren of Cornell I had never seen, although I had heard much about him and had read his writings, sent to me on board the steamer by the Committee for the Nation. While I do not agree with Dr. Warren's theory, and consider the practical steps he advocated in some respects almost ridiculous, let me say at the outset that I do believe in the complete sincerity of the man. Warren impressed me above all else as earnest and well-intentioned, anxious to help, but not eager for personal recognition, convinced, but not dogmatic or bumptious, as were so many others of the New Deal economists.

Warren, Rogers, and I spent a long evening in New York together and found that we had more in common than I had expected. In theory we were miles apart, but in practice, curiously enough, the distances were much smaller. Rogers, feeling that the sterling rate was the essential thing, agreed with me that stabilization by international agreement should be sought as quickly as possible. We differed in that he thought we must have a rate of $4.86 or higher, whereas I thought that such a rate would be difficult to maintain, because of the inherent strength of the dollar as compared to the pound.

Warren, feeling that the gold price was the essential thing, also was in favor of stabilization by international agreement, provided that the dollar would be sufficiently devalued to raise the price level and restore approximately the conditions of 1926. All three of us agreed that uncertainty as to our money policy was bad, and that we should eliminate as much of it as we could as soon as possible.

I was in favor of an immediate announcement that revaluation would ultimately be undertaken at not more than 75 per cent and not less than 65 per cent of the original parity, the dollar then being at about 69 to 70 per cent. Warren was inclined to agree with this suggestion in principle, but felt that the range should be lower. (As I remember, 58 to 68 per cent was the figure he tentatively suggested.) Inasmuch as Warren believed in solitary devaluation as a cure for our troubles, whereas I did not, but reluctantly recognized that we were definitely committed to the idea already, it was quite natural that he should want the range as low as possible, whereas I should seek to devalue as little as possible—because, unless all currencies were to be reappraised and revalued by international agreement, I feared that it would be impossible to hold the dollar down.

As to the ultimate monetary standard to be adopted, Warren believed in the commodity dollar theory, and hence wanted some sort of managed currency—managed in accordance with a price index by changing the gold content upwards and downwards. What Rogers believed in I honestly do not know. Warren, however, was prepared to admit that the commodity dollar idea contained many practical pitfalls and seemed not unwilling to consider a compromise that I suggested. This compromise consisted in saying substantially this:

"If, over a period of time, it appears that there really is a gold shortage, and that prices are depressed by such a gold shortage, then steps should be taken by international agreement to revalue currencies from time to time in terms of gold."

Perhaps I took too much for granted in assuming that I had convinced Warren that this was as far as we should go. Perhaps he later changed his mind. In any case, he plumped later on—and the President plumped with him—for a much more drastic application of the gold price theory. In the meantime the three of us went to Hyde Park and reported our agreements and disagreements.

The President was not at all impressed with our arguments in favor of a clear definition of our monetary policy. He wanted, above all else, to see commodity prices go up. He was interested—much more interested than I liked to see him—in the countless scrolls of tissue paper on which Warren had traced all sorts of curves and diagrams. The table was covered with them. Warren, expanding in the warmth of the President's enthusiasm, leaned over the table and explained the meaning of his cabalistic symbols. Rogers smiled enigmatically and from time to time nodded his head.

The meaning of Warren's charts and graphs—to Warren —was that the price of commodities went up and down automatically with the price of gold. Therefore all one had to do to control the price of commodities was to control the price of gold. To put up commodities one only had to put up the price of gold—which is the same thing as reducing the gold content of the dollar. The President was interested—had been interested for some time—in this alluringly simple idea.

I raised several objections. In the first place I pointed out that Warren's graphs represented only the prices of commodities with an international market. They did not show that milk or eggs or beef were affected by the ups and downs of the dollar in terms of gold.

In the second place, I tried to bring out the point that so

far the dollar's fluctuations in gold had corresponded almost exactly to its fluctuations in terms of foreign exchange rates, and that consequently Warren's charts made out just as good a case for the exchange rate as the controlling factor on commodity prices as for the gold price. In this I received support from Rogers. Warren, on the other hand, had contended that the exchange rate had little if anything to do with it.

I asked Warren whether, in his opinion, it was the domestic price for gold or the world price that governed domestic commodity prices. He said that it was the domestic price—that each country could regulate its commodity price level by regulating its gold price.

In that case, I said, all we have to do is to pay a higher price for newly mined domestic gold in order to put up wheat and cotton and so forth? Warren said he thought so. In any case, he thought we should try that first. If it did not work, then he was quite sure that putting up the world price of gold would do the trick.

I said to the President that, if he would do what Warren suggested about newly mined gold, I thought it would provide the proof of my contention that, while fluctuations of the dollar in the exchange market did influence the prices of international—although not all—commodities, the domestic price of gold would not influence anything except the position of the domestic gold miners. I said that in effect we should then have two dollars: one measured by the exchange rate, and the other measured by Warren's domestic gold thermometer; and that, in my opinion,

Warren's dollar would have no significance whatever. I pointed out, however, that to try such an experiment seemed to me undesirable, because it would make us look foolish, and that then there would be the temptation to try lifting the world price of gold.

Unfortunately there was a practical political element in Warren's favor, in that the domestic gold miners were clamoring for some sort of relief. Nevertheless, when we left, I felt that the President, while intrigued by Warren's ideas, was by no means convinced of them. The fact that he told both Warren and Rogers that he thought it would be useful for them to carry out their plans of going to Europe on a short trip added to my sense of security. And when shortly afterwards he authorized a group to study under Woodin's supervision the various elements of the monetary problem, it seemed as though there would be plenty of time to develop a carefully worked-out policy.

What this group did, who was in it, and what it finally recommended is a story which I do not feel free at the present time to tell. The group never had any official existence, and its reports, which did not endorse the Warren theory, were of an informal nature. They were submitted on about the 1st of September, and I think it is no exaggeration to say that they had no permanent influence on the President.

It is my own feeling that, even as late as September, the battle had not been definitely lost—nor had the President been convinced of the soundness of the Warren-Fisher-Committee-for-the-Nation-theory. It is my own feeling that if certain other things had not happened, he might never have decided to give this theory a trial. What these things were we shall see in the next chapter.

Note: I have avoided here going into a scientific refutation of the Warren gold theory. Many economists, more qualified to do so than I, have shown where its fundamental fallacy lies. I refer the reader who is interested to pursue the matter further to the following three pamphlets:

The Monetary Theories of Warren and Pearson
    by Walter E. Spahr (Farrar & Rinehart)
On the Practical Impossibility of a Commodity Dollar
    by Benjamin M. Anderson, Jr. (Chase National Bank)
Devaluation of the Dollar
    by Charles O. Hardy (University of Chicago Press)

CHAPTER XXI

Farm Revolt. "Come Michaelmas"

It is important to realize that the desire to raise prices, particularly farm prices, determined our monetary actions —far more than any purely monetary considerations.

Farm prices had been depressed much more than the general average of all prices. In March the "farm dollar"— that is, the dollar the farmer got for his products—was worth only about 68 per cent of the general dollar, in which he had to pay for seeds, machinery, clothes, and so forth. As we have seen, that was because a large part of the market for farm crops had vanished, while the acreage under cultivation was still as large as if the whole market were still there. In part this was due to smaller consumption within this country, but chiefly it was caused by the loss of our export markets, occasioned by the growth of nationalism throughout the world and the falling off of international trade.

By July the farm dollar had risen to about 74 per cent of the general dollar—that is, farm prices had risen considerably more than general prices. In part this was due to the hope of increased exports, to be made possible by the depreciation of our currency—in part to the prospects of smaller crops, under the agricultural program of production control—and in part to speculation in basic commodities, stimulated by the fear of inflation.

By the end of August, however, almost all of this gain in farm prices had been wiped out. Speculation came to an abrupt end in the July price crash. Sterling began to depreciate almost as fast as the dollar—which wiped out our export advantage as against the British Dominions. And doubt began to arise as to the effectiveness of the Agricultural Administration's methods of production control.

Beyond that, the N.R.A. had swung into action and through the imposition of its codes had begun to raise the cost of manufactured goods—in which the farmer was interested only as a purchaser. By September, therefore, the farmers were becoming exceedingly restless, since they saw not only the loss of their recent gain, but the probability that conditions would get even worse for them than they had been. This was not understood by many, because the prices of wheat and cotton were still much higher than they had been in March.

What people did not realize was that wheat and cotton were only a small part of the total farm crop, and that hogs, cattle, dairy products, and vegetables—which had no export market and did not benefit from depreciation of the dollar —were equally important, even though not quoted every day in the newspapers. And especially people did not realize that it was not merely farm prices in the abstract that interested the farmer, but the relation between farm prices and other prices.

This is one important factor on which it has always

seemed to me that our whole monetary policy—based on the Warren-Fisher-Committee-for-the-Nation doctrine—has broken down. Even if we assume that prices can be permanently raised by depreciating the currency—which I do not believe—no one has ever succeeded in showing me how, by depreciating the currency, we could hope to eliminate discrepancies within the general price level. And, as we have seen, it was the discrepancy between farm prices and other prices, rather than the general level of prices, which lay at the root of the farm trouble.

Let us pause here for a moment to register an opinion with which many may disagree. Quite irrespective of what may or may not be accomplished by manipulating money, prices cannot be raised permanently if the aggregate demand for commodities diminishes. Therefore, one of the most important factors influencing prices is the volume of trade—or, stated another way, the quantity of business which is done, and the profit at which it is done. The volume of business, in turn, cannot increase without confidence in money and without a free flow of investment funds into business for capital requirements, as well as a free flow of bank money and credit to finance turnover.

If you believe that—as I do and as most economists do—you cannot go very far in company with the monetary policy we adopted when the President announced his Warren gold-buying program in his radio broadcast of October 22. The reason you have to part company is very simple: you cannot see how such a program can provide the basis for the necessary confidence in money, or for the necessary flow of money, to bring about an increased volume of profitable turnover. And turnover, as we have seen, is what creates money and keeps it in circulation.

Now, what made the President go the other way? A belief that what I have just said is not true?

I may be entirely wrong, but I do not think so. I believe that what made him go the other way was the necessity for some sort of immediate action. If there had been no widespread distress, no threat of disorder arising from this distress, and, above all, no articulate and vociferous demand for inflation, I do not believe that he would have chosen the course he took.

I do not presume to judge whether the necessity was actually such as to compel him to this particular course. Certainly he was under great pressure to go much further in the direction of inflation than he did actually go. And if immediate spectacular action was really necessary, I am the first to admit that those of us who opposed Warren had no equally spectacular alternative to offer.

Here are a few of the ways in which necessity for action expressed itself.

On September 1st the dollar stood at about 70 cents. On September 8 the President issued an order permitting the sale of newly mined domestic gold through the Federal Reserve Banks to foreign buyers or to domestic licensed users in the arts and crafts. This enabled the gold miners to obtain the world price for gold, which was then $29.62, as against a previous mint price of $20.67 per ounce. A day afterwards the dollar rose to about 71½ cents, and a howl went up from those who wanted further depreciation.

The inflationists in Congress began to hold meetings and to issue statements. The Committee for the Nation clamored for a free gold market and a rapid marking up of the price of gold to $41.34, which would mean a fifty-cent dollar. Senator Thomas summoned the faithful. The wheat and cotton belts were not slow in responding. The commotion rose to an uproar—and on every street corner one man was asking another: "What will the President do about it?"

Under the influence of this inflationary talk, the dollar fell rapidly until it reached a low of 63¾ cents on September 18. That was the day on which a "Cotton Committee," with the approval of many Senators, adopted a memorial to the President favoring an increased issue of United States notes (greenbacks), praising Civil War currency inflation, and urging the establishment of a minimum price of twenty cents per pound for cotton. The committee asserted that cotton-price conditions were "worse today than have existed during this entire depression." (The price that day was 9⅞ cents as against 5¾ cents on February 4.)

The President kept the committee waiting for some time. Then he received them, but barred all talk of currency inflation. Instead, he offered the cotton-growers loans without liability at ten cents a pound.

This action was optimistically hailed by the anti-inflationists as a stand by the President against further depreciation. The dollar recovered two cents in the exchange markets. Stocks and commodities fell, as speculators shifted their positions.

On September 20 I made my last attempt to convince the President that further depreciation of the currency would do more harm than good. In a memorandum left with him that day, and in the course of discussion, I said in part:

"I believe that this is probably the last moment at which drastic inflation can be forestalled. The dollar has now been depreciated by 35 per cent, and whatever benefits could be derived from depreciation of the currency would seem to have been realized. A further depreciation, even if it can be controlled, would do vastly more harm than good. It would not only further impair the savings of the people, as represented by life-insurance policies, savings-bank accounts, or bonds, but would also destroy the purchasing power of the wage-earner. For example, the very wages fixed as minimums by the NRA a few weeks ago are already impaired by the depreciation of the dollar which has taken place since they were established.

"This is not a plea for capitalists. Capitalists by and large will be able to protect themselves to a certain extent. This is a plea for the man who lives on wages, or who has retired on the savings of past wages. It is the laboring class and the small bourgeoisie which will suffer most from here on, and the only one who will benefit is the speculator.

"Public opinion in favor of inflation has been aroused

and articulate. Nevertheless there is a latent public opinion, numerically far stronger, against inflation, which has not been aroused. It would not be difficult to make this opinion against inflation articulate.

"It is therefore recommended that steps be taken to arouse this dormant opinion, and that, at the proper time, a statement be issued from the White House to the effect that, in the judgment of the President, further depreciation of the currency would be undesirable and destructive, and that recovery from here on must be a gradual, orderly process, built upon sound enterprise, and fostered by a sound credit structure; that the efforts of the Administration will henceforth be directed towards freeing money that is frozen, rather than towards the artificial creation of more money, and towards the creation of such conditions as will attract money into normal business investment."

The President listened patiently to what I had to say, but when I was all through, he smiled and told me that all that was very pretty, but meantime how were we going to keep prices advancing? How were we going to relieve the debt burden? What were we going to do about the farmers?

It was then that I realized with a sense of finality how impossible it was to combat successfully a group of advisers who had ready answers to all these questions, while the only answers those of us could give who felt that the cure could not be a purely monetary one involved a slow and more or less painful process of rebuilding.

For the moment—but only for the moment—we had an immediate factor in our favor. There were large Government maturities and Government financing had to be done. An anti-inflation atmosphere was essential for the success of these operations.

On October 7 the dollar had risen to about 67½ cents. A day later the Treasury sold $75,000,000 ninety-one-day bills at a yield of less than ⅛ per cent per annum. On October 11 the Treasury called $1,900,000,000 Fourth Liberty Loan 4¼ per cent Bonds for redemption in April, and made a conversion offer into twelve-year bonds bearing interest for one year at 4¼ per cent and thereafter at 3¼ per cent. This operation was hailed here and abroad as a definite pledge by the Administration against an inflationary policy!

The dollar rose steadily until it reached almost 72 cents on the 20th of October. Meanwhile commodity prices and stocks were being liquidated at lower and lower prices. Wheat dropped over twenty-one cents a bushel, cotton dropped a cent a pound—the farmers in the Middle West were seething with revolt.

On the night of October 21 the die was cast. The President, in a radio broadcast, came out flatly for the program advocated by Warren and the Committee for the Nation. He announced his intention of raising prices by buying and selling gold, here, or abroad if necessary—of moving "toward a managed currency"—and of seeking "to establish and maintain a dollar which will not change its purchasing and debt-paying power during the succeeding generation."

The whole story was told in a few brief sentences uttered at the end of a speech on the general aspects of the recovery program:

"My aim in taking this step" (inaugurating gold purchases) "is to establish and maintain continuous control."

"This is a policy and not an expedient."

"We are thus continuing to move toward a managed currency."

As I heard these sentences, sitting in the house of a friend in Chicago, I felt much the same as on the night of April 18 in Washington and on the morning of July 3 in London.

The inflationists roared their delight. Wheat, cotton, and stocks soared upwards. The dollar dropped in lurches. On October 25 the new program went into effect, at a price of $31.36 per ounce as against $29.80 on the previous day and $28.50 on October 14. A 66-cent dollar as against a 72-cent dollar.

From then to the end of the month the price was arbitrarily advanced every business day. On the last day of the month it was $32.12, making the dollar worth 64.35 per cent of its old par—in terms of Warren's gold thermometer, but not in terms of anything else.

On the exchange market the very thing happened that many of us had foreseen. The dollar dropped under the psychological impact of the Administration's avowed intention to make it drop, but it did not drop according to Warren's daily gold figure. On the contrary, it stayed consistently two or three cents above Warren's figure.

There were now two dollars, a Warren dollar, and a foreign exchange dollar. And there was hopeless confusion in the minds of the people.

CHAPTER XXII

Bank Problems — "Sound" Money

We have been following the thread of gold and currency in tracing the development of Roosevelt's monetary policy. Before we continue this story through November, December, and the re-entrance of Congress upon the scene in January, let us see what in the meantime had been happening in the field of "bank money."

In a previous chapter we have seen how the Glass-Steagall Bill became law, without modification of its permanent guarantee plan, so that by July 1, 1934 all banks would become liable without known limit for each other's troubles. In the interim a temporary and limited guarantee plan was provided by the law, to go into effect on January 1, 1934. By this date, therefore, the qualifications for membership in the insurance plan would have to be determined, and all the banks would have to be examined in order to ascertain whether they could pass the requirements or not.

Having made itself morally responsible for the soundness of the banks reopened in March, and having chosen as a method of fulfilment the creation of a guarantee of deposits, the Government now faced the stupendous task of examining some 18,000 banks before the end of the year. Moreover, it was a foregone conclusion that practically all of the reopened institutions would have to be made eligible for the guarantee if the Government was to make good on its promise and if a second banking collapse was to be avoided.

There were two ways in which this could be done. The easiest way was to make the eligibility requirements so lax that almost all the banks could qualify. This could be done very simply by a generous appraisal of their frozen assets, but it would mean in the long run that no banks would be any good and that the Government would eventually have to take them all over.

The second alternative, which the Government wisely elected to follow, was to be rigorous in examination and appraisal of assets, but liberal in restoring impaired capital structures. This alternative, though vastly preferable to the first, also had its unpleasant features. It meant that the Reconstruction Finance Corporation would have to subscribe hundreds of millions of dollars to the capital structures of thousands of banks, which otherwise could not qualify. In other words, to make good its promise made in March, the Government was now compelled to go deeply into the banking business.

Throughout August and September the R. F. C. tried to find the weak spots, tried to effect reorganizations, tried to get stockholders of banks to put up at least part of the money that was needed. In some cases it succeeded; in others the stockholders had no money to put up; and everywhere the process showed itself as too slow to accomplish the result, which had to be accomplished by the end of year. Banks, even when they needed help, were reluctant to take it, because they feared the effect of Government participation upon their depositors.

Accordingly it soon became evident that the R. F. C. must proceed more rapidly and along more stereotyped lines. A drive was energetically put on by Jesse Jones, the R. F. C. chairman, to get all banks—even those that needed no help—to sell preferred stock or capital notes to the Government. By thus getting the banks whose capital was not impaired to take the Government into partnership, it was hoped to remove the hesitation being displayed by many of the banks who needed help most. In general this plan was successful. By the end of the year Jesse Jones and the army of examiners under the Comptroller of the Currency and the state superintendents of banks had done their job. The temporary plan went into effect on January 1, 1934. 13,341 open banks had been examined and had qualified; 141 had been rejected. 1,396 had not applied. The R. F. C. had invested or agreed to invest almost a billion dollars in the capital structures of over 6,000 banks. (44 per cent of the banks opened without restriction.) Over $40,000,000,000 of "bank money" was again free to circulate.

The public was safe for the time being. But the Government was in the banking business. And the question of the permanent plan still overhung the banking structure.

Meanwhile the Senate investigation had been proceeding, and had served to stress more than ever the necessity for real banking reform. With this problem we shall deal in Part III.

And now we can return to the thread of our gold and price story.

All through November the Government's experiment in gold manipulation continued. Except for two intervals of four days each, the price was advanced on each business day, from $32.12 to $33.93 at the end of the month. According to the Warren theory this brought the value of the dollar down to 60.92 cents, but in the exchange market the dollar stood at almost 64 cents. By this time it was evident that marking up the gold price on a blackboard each day had little or no significance, and the Committee for the Nation was clamoring for a widening of the policy to purchases of gold abroad. This, they said, would make the gold price effective, because it would raise the world price for gold. I did not see Warren during this time, but I am told that he too was now convinced that it was not the domestic price for gold, but the world price that would do the trick.

To make matters worse, in spite of all the ballyhoo and the daily publicity given to the gold price changes, commodity prices had not only failed to go up with the gold price—they had actually gone down. At the close of November the Bureau of Labor's index stood at 70.7, as against 70.9 in the week of October that saw the beginning of the experiment.

Nor was there any cheer in the picture for Dr. Rogers, who believed that the sterling-dollar rate rather than the gold price was the determining factor upon our price level. Sterling, depreciating more slowly than the dollar, ran up in dollars to $5.52 per pound, and yet commodities failed to rise. It was a trying time for the money doctors.

Meanwhile all the markets were in a state of complete confusion. Here and there throughout the country little knots of business men gathered in groups to see if they could help each other to understand what was going on. There was much shaking of heads, and, for the first time, people began to criticize openly.

The American Federation of Labor went on record against inflation. So did the American Legion. A group of economists in Chicago published a strong statement against the President's monetary policy and called for the abandonment of currency experimentation. This was followed by the organization of a Committee on Monetary Policy, which issued the following statement of policy:

1. Recovery can be achieved only through an increased volume of business, which increases wages and the whole national income.

2. The fundamental condition for an increased volume of business is confidence in the dollar and in the national credit, and a reasonable expectation of profit for individual enterprise, in industry, in trade, in agriculture.

3. Confidence in the dollar and in the national credit demands that currency experimentation be abandoned, and that depreciation of the currency be stopped before it gets out of hand.

4. A higher price level is desirable only if accompanied by increased income—for farmers, wage-earners, and

business men, big and little—and this cannot be achieved by manipulation of our currency.

5. Further depreciation of the dollar by Government action is the road to printing press money, which means the further disorganization of agricultural and industrial production, and the ultimate impoverishment of the nation—of its wage-earners, its farmers, and of every individual citizen, debtor and creditor alike.

6. An announced determination to return to a fixed gold standard, giving effect to current needs and experience, is indispensable to the elimination of uncertainty and to the restoration of confidence in the dollar.

The New York Chamber of Commerce passed a resolution urging the return to a gold standard. Others followed throughout the country. Various economists, singly and in groups, voiced their criticism. Acheson resigned as Undersecretary of the Treasury, and Morgenthau supplanted him. Sprague resigned and did not hesitate to say why. The Advisory Council of the Federal Reserve Board and the United States Chamber of Commerce added their voices to the "sound money" chorus. At a meeting of the American Academy of Political and Social Science in Philadelphia I delivered my own first public protest in a reply to Professor Fisher and Senator Thomas.

The "sound money" crusade reached its high-water mark on November 24, when Al Smith wheeled up the heavy guns of his picturesque vocabulary and blasted the "crackpots" and "quarterbacks" in Washington, who were turning "130,000,000 Americans into guinea-pigs for experimentation." That did the "sound money" cause more harm than good. So far it had been conducted along coldly scientific lines. The oratory had been left to the inflationists. Al Smith brought in the element of personal criticism, and it bounced back off the wall of the President's impregnable popularity.

During these weeks of public clamor against the gold-buying policy little was heard from the inflationists. They seemed cowed and a little uncertain. One voice alone went steadily on preaching the gospel, a curiously electrifying voice, even if one disagrees with it—the voice of Father Coughlin. And when the Sound Money Committee of the Crusaders hired Carnegie Hall for a mass meeting, at which Matthew Woll of the A. F. of L. and others were to speak, Father Coughlin got his friends to arrange a counter mass meeting at the Hippodrome and came on from Detroit to address it. Whether one agrees with Coughlin or not (and I do not), whether one likes or dislikes his methods (and I dislike them), one must unhesitatingly give him full credit for turning the tide of popular opinion at this critical juncture. In less than half an hour of blazing oratory he undid months of hard work by the opposition. If history shows that the President's monetary program was worth saving, Father Coughlin deserves much of the credit for saving it.

Personally, I doubt whether history will accord much merit to the whole Warren-Committee-for-the-Nation policy, or to any of its supporters. And I believe that

Franklin Roosevelt will get more credit, when the final page is written, for having resisted inflation than for the steps he took in its direction.

By contrast, December was a relatively quiet month. Whether because of the widespread criticism or because results failed to justify its continuance, the Government abandoned its efforts to raise the gold price any further. During the whole month the price was raised only once, from $34.01 to $34.06 on December 18. Commodities declined a little. Security markets were fairly steady. Sterling fell to about $5.05 and seemed to hang there. There was a general atmosphere of waiting to see what would happen when Congress met in January.

Silver furnished the only excitement of the month. On December 21 the President suddenly announced ratification of the international silver agreement, worked out by Senator Pittman in London. This was no particular surprise. But he announced also a buying program for newly mined domestic silver, which was at first glance just as baffling as the gold program. What this step amounted to, when analyzed in the cold light of day, was nothing but a sop to the silver interests.

By agreeing to buy newly mined silver (domestic only) at 64½ cents per ounce, as against a market price of about 43½ cents, the President made life pleasant for the silver miners, and thus to a certain extent drew the fangs of the silver enthusiasts in Congress. The effect upon the silver market was negligible, and the silver faction in Congress was pleased for only a very short time.

Throughout the month criticism of the monetary policy continued from various sources. But the public had lost interest. There was a mild flare-up of excitement when, on the last day of the year, J. Maynard Keynes, who had earlier pronounced Roosevelt "magnificently right," came out with a stinging criticism. Keynes, upon whom Fisher and Warren leaned heavily for support, described the "gyrations of the dollar" under the Government's manipulation as "more like a gold standard on the booze" than an ideally managed currency.

And, horror of horrors for Warren, he characterized as "foolish" the idea "that there is a mathematical relation between the price of gold and the price of other things."

CHAPTER XXIII

Congress Dances

Two questions were uppermost in people's minds as the new year opened; how far would the President continue to control Congress? And what would he recommend to Congress in regard to the Budget and money mechanism?

Just before Congress adjourned in June it had shown certain signs of becoming restive under the continued demands of the Executive for instantaneous action in many directions. Because of this the President had refrained from asking for power to negotiate tariff treaties, and in so doing had sent the American Delegation to London under a severe handicap.

Also because of this the President had accepted the Glass-Steagall Bill without the modifications which it urgently needed. During the recess many Congressional leaders had been more than usually active—particularly the silver group and the other inflationists—and it seemed doubtful whether Congress would be as docile in January as it had been in the previous spring.

As to the Budget, there was considerable doubt and apprehension. Three billion three hundred million dollars had been appropriated for Public Works. In addition there were Civil Works, Reforestation Camps, R. F. C. loans to banks and investments in banks, R. F. C. loans to railroads, loans to cotton-growers, purchases of wheat, purchases of gold, the farm program, mortgage relief, and so on—all running into hundreds of millions of dollars. No one knew exactly what it would all foot up to or how the money was to be found.

The currency and bank problems we have already discussed. Here again no one knew just how far the President intended to go with devaluation and a managed currency. Some said that Warren was already discredited, while others maintained that the President had slowed up the program in December only because he lacked the necessary legislative authority.

The answers were not long in coming.

In his message "on the state of the Union," delivered on the opening day of Congress, the President disclosed very little of his plans. What he did do was to make a brilliant appeal to Congress and the nation at large for continued support of his policies. Once again he wooed and won the whole-hearted allegiance of an overwhelming majority. One phrase in his message seemed significant; it related to the currency.

"We seek," he said, "a medium of exchange which will have over the years less variable purchasing and debt-paying power for our people than that of the past."

That seemed like a considerable retreat from the "dollar of constant purchasing and debt-paying power." To vary less is one thing; to vary not at all, quite another. One might mean an improved gold standard; the other had to mean, if it meant anything, a commodity dollar.

No sooner had he made sure of the temper of Congress than the President sent along his Budget Message. Without doubt this was one of the most amazing documents of its kind ever sent to a legislative body. Very calmly, in the most matter-of-fact tones, President Roosevelt informed Congress and the country that the deficit for this fiscal year would be about seven billion dollars; that for next year it would be about two billions; that ten billions would have to be borrowed within the next six months; that by June 30, 1935 the national debt would be about thirty-two billions; and that from there on, with luck, we might have a balanced budget!

Scarcely a word about increasing taxes to meet these extraordinary expenditures, and scarcely a word of justification for the whole program!

The President said in effect (these are not his words):

"You and I know perfectly well that there is no use in talking much about it. We have got to take care of unemployment. We have got to get agriculture and business back on their feet. We have worked out a program to do it, and that program will cost a lot of money. If it succeeds, you can well afford the taxes that will be necessary to retire the huge debt we shall have incurred. If it fails, our goose is so cooked anyway that a little more or a little less debt won't matter. There is no sense in hedging our bets. Play it on the nose, and pray that you have picked the right horse."

That is what, to my mind, the Budget Message really

said to Congress and to the country. And Congress and the country, in perhaps the most extraordinary vote of confidence ever given, gulped for a day or so, swallowed the pill, and cheerfully accepted the consequences. Whether the Roosevelt program leads us to recovery or chaos, to widespread prosperity or national ruin, let no one say that Roosevelt lacked the courage of his convictions—let no one say that the American people failed to recognize and support a cheerful and indomitable leader.

Sure of Congress, sure of the people, and with the bad news of the budget out of the way, the President next sent to Congress his long-awaited monetary message. In brief, it made three major recommendations:

1. that all monetary gold be taken over by the Treasury,
2. that the limits of revaluation be fixed between 50 and 60 per cent of the old dollar, and
3. that a large part of the "profit" due to revaluing gold be set aside as a stabilization fund, to steady the dollar and the national credit.

In the House of Representatives a row broke out—not over the substance of the Bill submitted by the White House shortly after his message, but between two committees, each of which claimed jurisdiction over the proposed measure.

Speaker Rainey awarded the bill to the Committee on Coinage, which had already proceeded to hold hearings. But Steagall, Chairman of the Banking and Currency Committee, reported the bill out anyway, by a parliamentary trick, so that the Coinage Committee cut short its hearings and likewise reported the bill favorably.

Thus the only real argument in the Lower House took place, not over one of the most far-reaching measures ever submitted to that body, but over which of two committees was to have the honor of voting aye first.

When the bill reached the floor, there were a few strong speeches made in opposition, but the measure passed by a vote of 360 to 40.

The Senate proceedings were a little more dignified, and preserved some semblance of a sense of legislative responsibility. The Senate Banking and Currency Committee held more extensive hearings, suggested certain amendments, and clearly was reluctant to recommend the bill. Two ex-Secretaries of the Treasury, Glass and McAdoo, brought home to the Committee the grave nature of some features of the measure. The vote in the Committee was close, and resulted in favor of the bill, largely, I think, because the Committee members knew that there was an overwhelming majority in the Senate which would set aside any unfavorable Committee report.

I was asked to testify before both committees—before the House Coinage Committee on January 17, and before the Senate Committee on Banking and Currency on January 20. My statement before the House Committee was made after reading the President's message, and after spending the previous evening at the White House, but before seeing the actual Gold Reserve Bill submitted to Congress. This statement appears in the appendix.

A careful study of the proposed bill destroyed much of

the feeling I had had before reading it, that the President was now definitely steering towards monetary stability. Moreover, Frank Vanderlip, apparently back in the arms of the Committee for the Nation, came out with a plan for the creation of a Federal Monetary Authority, which would completely kill the Federal Reserve System and put the power to create money under purely political control. He made specific the demand for "nationalization of the currency and banking system" which Father Coughlin had been proclaiming for months in general terms.

Accordingly, when testifying before the Senate, I felt compelled to point out what seemed to me the dangerous elements in the proposed measure, and also to answer the suggestion of a Federal Monetary Authority. The statements I made follow:

GENTLEMEN:

Two days ago I testified before the House Committee on Coinage, Weights and Measures. I prepared for this Committee a short general analysis of the monetary problem and a compilation of supplementary statements. I have sent printed copies of both to every member of Congress. At this hearing I commented upon the President's monetary message and was asked to comment upon the Bill S.2366 which is now before you. I could not then comment upon the Bill because I had not seen it.

I now have studied the Bill, and should like to make the following observations:

1. To all intents and purposes it seems to me that the

Bill endows the Secretary of the Treasury with most of the powers usually vested in a government note-issuing institution and with several other powers as well. To some extent this is doubtless necessary in an emergency, but I see nothing in the Bill to limit it to an emergency.

One cannot precisely define what constitutes an emergency. But one can define one's ultimate aim. I believe the Bill could be improved if it were made to state that our purpose is to return to a fixed ratio to gold, and that to this end we seek the establishment of an improved international gold standard. (I have set forth a detailed proposal for an improved gold standard in my published letters to Senator Borah and in my testimony before the House Committee.) If our ultimate aim were so defined, the powers conferred upon the Secretary of the Treasury could then be made to lapse when this ultimate aim is realized.

2. It seems to me that the Bill should state that it is not the intention to take the note-issuing power away from the Reserve System in whole or in part. Personally, I should like to see the Bill amended so as to contain an outright repeal of the "greenback section" of the Thomas Amendment, *the mere existence of which, to my mind, constitutes a menace to the National credit*. It will be difficult enough to keep expenditure within the limits of bearable taxation. The success of our program depends upon not over-straining the Government credit. The best barometer of strain on Government credit is the market for Government bonds. Support of this market by a stabilization fund may in moments of extreme emergency be necessary, but it must be

recognized that such support is tampering with the barometer. The issuance of Thomas Amendment notes would not be tampering with the barometer, but smashing it.

3. I expressed before the House Committee my views as to the danger of attempting to set too low a range for the dollar. I do not believe in the whole theory of raising prices by depreciating a currency, but, having embarked upon this theory for better or worse, I do believe that Congress should now support the President in carrying out his purpose. He has reached his conclusion as to the range within which stabilization is to take place, after the most careful consideration of all the circumstances. We are in his hands and we should strengthen his hands. That is why, in spite of a personal conviction that the range selected is too low, I do not urge altering it.

4. It seems to me that the Bill contains the elements of a drastic change of the Federal Reserve System. I have said that I believed the Government should take the "profit" from devaluation, but I question gravely the advisability of taking the Reserve Banks' gold and giving them gold certificates, which are only convertible into gold at the option of the Secretary of the Treasury, and in an amount of gold to be fixed by him. I believe that monetary gold should be owned directly by the note-issuing authority and that the note-issuing authority should not be purely under political control nor yet purely under private control, but should be vested in an institution owned partly by the public—not necessarily the banks—and partly by the Government. I believe that our Reserve System and our whole private

banking system are in need of careful and thorough over-hauling, but I do not think that this can be done by rushing through an emergency bill.

5. Finally, if money lies at the root of our economic troubles, which I for one think is only partially true, then, as ninety per cent of our money is check money, it would seem to me that ninety per cent of the cure of our money ills must lie in a properly reconstituted banking system, rather than in any measure that deals purely with the metallic base and the paper circulating medium.

Special Note for the Committee Concerning the Central Bank Problem

I do not believe it is wise to give the note-issuing power to any purely political body, even to such a permanent body as Mr. Vanderlip has suggested. Nor do I believe that the note-issuing power should be vested in a private corporation. There is the danger of control or abuse by "big business," which must be avoided, just as much as the danger of political abuse must be avoided. That is what our Federal Reserve Act attempted to do. I believe that we can improve the Federal Reserve Act, and that we should do so, but only after the most careful study—and not as an emergency job to be done in a few days.

Concretely I would suggest tentatively two ideas:

I. A change in the composition of the Board, so that it would consist of three appointed members,—a Governor, a Vice-Governor, and a Secretary General. These three officials to be appointed for long terms and to receive much higher salaries than at present. (This involves no additional expense, because the salaries of three members are saved.) The Governor and Vice-Governor each to have two votes.

In addition to the three appointed members, four out of the twelve Federal Reserve Bank Governors would compose the Board. The Governors would serve in rotation, for six-month periods, which means that each Bank Governor would serve as a Board member for six months in every eighteen.

This would have the following advantages:

A. The higher salaries would help to engage the best possible men.

B. The present conflict between Board and Banks would be largely eliminated.

C. It would necessitate having at least one strong Deputy-Governor in each Reserve Bank.

II. The other idea, which I would put forward tentatively, is that it would be better to have the ownership of the Reserve Banks in the public, rather than in the banks of the country. One might consider having two classes of stock—one held by the public, and the other by the Government. The public's stock would have limited voting rights, and a limited return, while the Government's stock would receive the bulk of the profits after the public had received a fair minimum dividend. There are any number of possible variations to such a scheme—many of them have been in use. I should not want to make a specific suggestion without studying all the available material, but I do wish to record my opinion now that this line of thought seems to me more fruitful than the creation of a Government note-issuing authority. And I also think that ownership by the public direct is more in line with present-day thought than ownership through the private banks.

JAMES P. WARBURG

January 20, 1934

A few days later Owen D. Young said much the same thing—more ably and more in detail.

When the Bill reached the floor of the Senate, little Carter Glass fought like a tiger, even though he was so sick that he could scarcely stand up.

The silver bloc tried to tack on a 16-to-1 silver amendment and failed by only two votes. Pittman got an amendment accepted which gave the President power to buy silver anywhere in the world at any price up to $1.29 per ounce.

There was a scattering fusillade of Republican firing. And then the Senate majestically lay down and rolled over by a vote of 66 to 23.

Congress had abdicated. The power over money was now solely in the hands of the Executive.

PART THREE

AND NOW WHAT DO WE DO?

CHAPTER XXIV

Jump, Cat, Jump

THE NATIONAL CURRENCY

The Gold Reserve Bill went to the President on January 30, 1934. The President signed it a day later, and issued a proclamation formally devaluing the dollar to 59.06 per cent of its old par value. This rather curious figure was arrived at by fixing the price of gold at exactly $35.00 an ounce (as against the old mint price of $20.67). The method was significant, because it deliberately stressed the importance of the gold price and the unimportance of the new dollar's relation to the old parity.

Once more there was considerable confusion in the exchange markets. Some said that this meant we were back on a gold basis at a new ratio. Others pointed out that the President could—and probably would—change the gold price again, whenever it seemed desirable to do so.

The Treasury issued new gold regulations, which permitted anyone to sell gold to the Government at the new price, provided he could show that it was not illegally hoarded gold. That meant that it became profitable to buy gold abroad and bring it in, just as long as it could be bought abroad at less than about $34.70 per ounce. (The cost of shipping, interest, and insurance amounts to about 25 cents per ounce.)

A gold rush started. American banks began to buy gold in London, Paris, Amsterdam, Bombay, or South Africa—anywhere they could lay hands on it. In four weeks something like four hundred million dollars' worth of the metal was brought into this country, and more would have been brought if the ships had been available. As I write this, in early March, the yellow tide is still pouring in, though not so swiftly, because two things have happened:

Some of the gold countries, such as Holland, have put restrictions on the export of gold in order to protect their dwindling gold reserves. France is moving slowly in the same direction. And in the "off-gold" countries the price of gold has been allowed to rise so as to meet our price and thus make exports of gold to the United States no longer profitable.

Put the other way round, this means that Great Britain has allowed the pound to drop off in terms of gold, in order to compensate for the depreciation of the dollar. That stops drainage of English gold to the United States, but it causes shipments to England as well as to the United States from the "gold countries"—provided they let the gold continue to flow out.

Obviously it cannot take very long before the rest of the world calls a halt in this procedure.

Then where are we?

Under the Gold Reserve Act we have set up a stabilization fund of two billion dollars, by setting aside that much of the "profit" we made through revaluing the gold stocks of the Treasury and the Federal Reserve System. Later we shall come to the question of gold ownership. For the moment we are concerned with the stabilization fund.

The fund is in the hands of the Secretary of the Treasury, to use in his sole discretion. There was an attempt made in the Senate to create a board of five members, but this suggestion was turned down by the President. Henry Morgenthau, successor to William Woodin, pupil of George Warren, therefore has in his hands this gigantic sum of money —as well as the gigantic job of managing the dollar by means of it.

What is Henry Morgenthau going to do?

So far his job has been done for him—by the workings of the gold standard, and at the expense of the gold standard countries.

Obviously this puts a strain on the gold reserves of the "gold countries" that will sooner or later force them to embargo gold shipments or devalue their currencies. Then the job of holding the dollar to 59.06 per cent of its old parity will become something more than the spectator's job it has been so far.

It is always foolish to indulge in the temptation to prophesy. At a time like this, and in relation to so complicated a problem, it would be ridiculous to attempt to do so. All one can say at the moment—and even this may be wrong—is that there are certain possibilities that bear careful thinking. For instance:

If, by reason of embargoes, gold shipments cease, it will be perfectly simple to maintain our gold price of thirty-five dollars per ounce, but it will not be at all simple to keep the dollar at any particular ratio to the pound, or to any other currencies.

If Mr. Morgenthau (that is, the President) feels that Professor Warren is right, and that the gold price is all that matters, then there is no particular reason to worry about exchange rates. But I suspect that a four-dollar pound would scarcely suit the President's program of raising prices by depreciating the currency. I suspect that if gold shipments stopped, and if the pound were to drop from about five dollars, which it is now, to about $4.50, one of two things would happen:

We should either boost the gold price some more—which is what the Committee for the Nation is already screaming for—or we should start to sell dollars abroad and buy foreign currencies.

If we boost the gold price, but no more gold is allowed to come to this country, I should expect that nothing at all would happen to further Mr. Morgenthau's purpose. We should of course store up an even greater danger of ultimate uncontrolled inflation than we have already. We should probably weaken our dollar somewhat in the exchange markets by frightening people once more, but an exchange rate cannot be permanently controlled by a series of psychological shocks and counter-shocks.

We should then come to the second alternative—namely, that we should start in to purchase foreign currencies in the hope of holding down the dollar. The dangers of such a course are almost too obvious to require elaboration. On the one hand we should almost certainly see other countries doing the same thing, thereby nullifying our efforts. And on the other hand the operation would entail the same stupid risks that are inherent in any attempt to manipulate any market contrary to the natural forces of demand and supply.

That is why, whether we first have to go through a currency war or not, I cannot see how we shall ever arrive at a sensible conclusion without eventual international co-operation. If that is true, it has always seemed to me that the sooner we co-operate, the better for all concerned.

Often I have heard it claimed that England and Sweden have been very successful in managing their currencies to suit themselves, and "if they can, why can't we?"

Because England "managed," as I have said before, by means of the gold standard, using as the fulcrum for her lever the countries that were still on the gold standard. That little game is practically over now, and from here on, England will have much the same mechanical problem of "management" that we have—without, however, being burdened with a preconceived notion as to raising prices and bringing about recovery through currency depreciation.

Sweden "managed" by the simple method of pegging its krona to the pound, which in turn was raising and lowering itself by means of the gold standard.

Once the gold standard mechanism is completely gone, exchange rates—prices of one currency in terms of other currencies—will have to depend purely upon the balance of payments between the various countries. In other words, they will depend upon demand and supply.

Our balance of payments is favorable. Others must buy more dollars than we must buy foreign exchanges. Once the gold standard mechanism ceases to operate, Mr. Morgenthau will have quite a little problem, if he decides that the dollar should stay below where our balance of payments wants to put it. And I personally believe that Washington tends to underestimate the relative strength of our currency.

Of course, there are things we can do to change our balance of payments. We can reduce our exports. We can lower tariffs and increase our imports. We can resume foreign lending operations. We can cancel war debts. But all these things are difficult, and at best require time, while Mr. Morgenthau's problem of holding down the dollar threatens to be immediate.

There are also other things we can do to reduce the inherent strength of our dollar. We can print greenbacks, or have free coinage of silver, or run up a huge debt without providing for its retirement. But those things lead to a destruction of the value of our currency and are dangerous tools to use, if all we want is to hold the dollar down. And, again, even these methods take time.

So we see that Henry Morgenthau has a problem, and we see various things that may happen.

Only one thing is certain:

Anything that is artificial, anything that represents interference by force with the laws of supply and demand, will not be of lasting benefit. We can change demand. We can change supply. We can, by artificialities, defer the action of demand and supply. But we can no more change the law of nature than we can drop a thousand feet without a parachute and not be killed.

So much for the stabilization fund, in so far as it has to do with the currency. Its use to support Government bonds is a subject which belongs in a following chapter.

Before we leave the subject of currency, let us see what else has happened by reason of the Gold Reserve Act.

First I should like to mention two things that have not happened, and that, to my mind, should have happened.

In the first place, nothing has been decided as to our ultimate aim in money. There has been no indication as to whether we are moving toward the re-establishment of an improved international gold standard, or toward a commodity dollar.

The Gold Reserve Act fixes an upper and lower limit of revaluation. It limits the President's discretion to a top of sixty per cent and a bottom of fifty per cent of the old par dollar. But it does not provide that somewhere between these two points a fixed ratio to gold is to be re-established. Under the law the President may, if he chooses, revalue the dollar any number of times between the two limits laid down.

From the point of view of the immediate future there is no harm in giving the President this power. In fact, if we are to revalue intelligently, we can only do so after a certain amount of trial and error and after international trade and currency agreements have provided some assurance of a proper redistribution and functioning of gold. But if this arrangement is to be a permanent one, that is another story.

I can see no reason why there should be so much mystery about our ultimate purpose. If we seek to re-establish a fixed ratio to gold somewhere between the two limits set, why not say so?

That would eliminate much of the uncertainty that now stands in the way of progress. No reasonable person could expect the President to go back to a fixed ratio until the necessary international agreements had been reached. I for one should like to see him keep his hands free until at least the sterling countries are ready to co-operate and return to a gold standard. But that is no reason to conceal our ultimate intention—if that is our intention.

If, on the other hand, the President does not desire to go back eventually to a fixed ratio to gold—if he wants to have a dollar of variable gold content—that is, a commodity dollar—why not let that purpose become known?

Because there would be a storm of protest and criticism? I should indeed hope that there would be such a storm, but if the Administration is convinced of the soundness of the idea, why not have the criticism now and meet it or be convinced by it? The test will have to come some time.

Furthermore, if the commodity dollar is the ultimate objective, the present law is absurdly inadequate. If you are going to have a dollar of variable gold content in order to have a more constant purchasing power, it seems to me that you have to go the whole way. You can't stop arbitrarily at a fifty-cent dollar if prices continue downwards, any more than you can stop arbitrarily at a sixty-cent dollar if prices continue upwards.

This is so obvious that it makes me read into the law an intention to go back to a fixed ratio to gold—at the proper time and under the proper conditions. But if that is our intention, as I devoutly hope it is, why not say so?

The second thing that failed to happen when the Gold Reserve Bill was passed was a repeal of the greenback section of the Thomas Amendment. If it was the intention to move toward currency stability, it is impossible for me to conceive of leaving the issuance of greenbacks an open question.

When I said this to the Senate Committee on Banking and Currency, Senator Gore remarked:

"You might as well try to repeal the law of gravitation!" (meaning, of course, that it was hopeless to try to get such action through Congress at this time). Perhaps it would have been hopeless, but why not try?

The attempt would go far toward showing what the Administration believed in, and what it hoped to do. There are plenty of people who are in doubt today who would then have said: "Oh, there won't be any greenbacks. Not while Roosevelt is President."

Of course, there would have been plenty of others who would have roared their anger, because they want greenbacks.

But again, why not face the issue now?

I am not a politician, and I do not pretend to any knowledge of politics. I have been told that the sort of thing I have just been saying is rubbish from a political point of view. Perhaps it is. But I cannot help feeling that the average citizen, who knows just as little about politics as I do, would feel a lot happier if he knew a little more about our ultimate objectives—even if he disagreed with some of them.

Apart from what the Gold Reserve Act did not do, it did do one other thing, the wisdom of which seems to me highly doubtful.

It took away the Federal Reserve System's gold in exchange for something which is called, but is not, a gold certificate.

If there was to be a revaluation of gold, there can be no question that the Government, and not the Federal Reserve Banks, should capture the "profit." Many people think otherwise, but in that respect I agree thoroughly with the Administration.

It does not follow, however, that the Government should seize the original gold holdings of the Federal Reserve Banks as well as the "profit."

One of the major functions of the Federal Reserve System is to create our paper currency. (We still have, as the left-over remains of previous currency systems, national bank notes, silver certificates, a small amount of greenbacks, and so forth. But since 1914 our national currency was primarily Federal Reserve currency.)

The Federal Reserve Act was the product of years of study and centuries of experience. It was not perfect. No legislation ever is. But it laid down certain principles, which were, and still are, recognized as wise safe-guards.

One of these principles was a legal minimum "gold cover." We have discussed this in a previous chapter (see page 25).

A second principle was that of "commercial paper cover" for that part of the note circulation not covered by gold. This also we have discussed (see page 36).

A third principle was that of mixed ownership and control of the note-issuing authority, so as to avoid the dangers of political or business abuse. We have seen how that lesson was learned from bitter experience (see page 25).

The Gold Reserve Act strikes at the heart of these principles, and, in so doing, strikes at the heart of the Federal Reserve System.

The worst of it is that the Gold Reserve Act does not set up a new system in place of the old. Setting up a new system might be a good thing—if the new system were a better one. It sets up nothing at all, except a lot of powers placed in the hands of the Secretary of the Treasury—and a lot of question-marks.

There is no need to go deeply into technical detail. Here is an example of what I mean by question-marks.

Do you know of what the "gold cover" behind the money in your pocket consists at the present time? No?

It consists of so-called "gold certificates," issued by the Secretary of the Treasury to the Federal Reserve Banks in exchange for the gold they used to hold. These certificates are not, as you might suppose, warehouse certificates for gold—or, rather, they are, but they are a funny kind of warehouse certificate. They are a warehouse certificate for an amount of gold to be determined by the Secretary of the Treasury, whenever he thinks it is a good idea to determine it.

It is just as if I said:

"You put four dozen eggs in my warehouse and I will give you a receipt for eggs. Not four dozen eggs. Just eggs."

That is not all. Under the terms of this "gold certificate" the Secretary of the Treasury, in his sole discretion, determines whether the Federal Reserve Banks may get any gold at all for their certificates.

So it is not even a receipt for just eggs. It is for eggs—maybe.

Do you see what I mean by question-marks?

Here is another one.

Before the ink was dry on the proposed bill, it was being attacked from various quarters because it did not go far enough. Mr. Vanderlip and the Committee for the Nation demanded the creation of a "Federal Monetary Authority," which Vanderlip, testifying before the Senate, said would not kill the Federal Reserve System, but would probably let it die slowly![1]

So far the Administration apparently does not want anything of that sort. But there is going to be a lot of propa-

---

[1] Senator Glass: "You would abolish the Federal Reserve System bodily then, would you?"

Mr. Vanderlip: "Oh, no. I would let its duties somewhat decrease, perhaps, and maybe it would abolish itself in time, but I would not interfere with it."

ganda for it. That is why I call the life of the Federal Reserve System one of the big question-marks.

Father Coughlin—when he is not boosting silver, or advocating symmetalism, or just cursing bankers in general—is fond of talking about "nationalizing our currency," whatever that means.

There are plenty of people in Washington who want to see the Treasury put out its own currency in one form or another. The neatest device is this:

"Why shouldn't the Treasury issue non-interest-bearing Treasury notes in currency denominations, with a forty per cent gold cover? That would be 'sound currency,' and we have enough gold now to issue billions of it."

If anyone says that to you, ask them what secures the other sixty per cent of such money.

Nothing secures it. Absolutely nothing.

And the necessary relation between money and business turnover is lost, because such money has no relation to the volume of commercial credit.

Ask them also whether they like the idea of purely political control of the creation of money.

Ask them whether they think any political government ever has or ever will put on the brakes in a boom period.

Ask them by what means the Government could, if it wanted to, put on the brakes.

Ask them anything you like, but don't let them tell you that such money is not sixty per cent greenback.

Finally, and this is the biggest question-mark of all in regard to our national currency:

We have gone far down the road recommended by the Committee for the Nation. We have taken far-reaching action on the theory propounded by Professor Warren. We have given no little encouragement to the silver enthusiasts and have kept the door open even to the greenbackers.[1] We have substituted for the Federal Reserve System a one-man currency dictatorship—not for a period of emergency, but more or less until further notice.

But we have not yet gone far enough to satisfy the inflationists by any means.

How far are we going with Messrs. Rumely, Rand, Vanderlip, Thomas, LeBlanc, and Father Coughlin?

If we are moving forward, what is our objective?

If we are in retreat before the inflationists, where do we stop retreating to dig in and fight?

---

[1] On March 13 the House passed the Patman Bonus Bill by an overwhelming majority, knowing that the President was committed to veto the measure.

On March 15 the New York *Times* printed a Washington dispatch as follows:

"His [the President's] position is that there is a great difference between the issuance of 'Baby Bonds' of small denominations to retire governmental issues and the printing of paper money unsecured to meet the current obligations of the Government. The former he believes is dangerous only in that it might tend to get Congress in the habit of repeating such issue year after year."

The significant thing about this statement is not that the President opposes issuing greenbacks to defray expenditure, but that he sees no harm—except for the bad habit that might result—in retiring Government bonds by printing Baby Bonds. "Baby Bonds" if they are non-interest-bearing and issued in small denominations for the retirement of Government obligations are in effect greenbacks. The distinction that they are not greenbacks because they would be "amortized" out of a budget does not seem to me in any sense valid. The original Greenback Act of 1862 also provided for "amortization."

CHAPTER XXV

Our Banking System, If Any

If we are to follow the school of thought that has dominated our monetary thinking in the past year, we must believe that money lies at the root of our troubles, and that hence the cure is to be found by altering the money structure. But, as we have seen, by far the greatest part of our money mechanism does not consist of gold or paper currency. It consists of "bank money."

Since this is true, it is difficult to see how any measures which deal solely with gold and paper currency can hope to bring about a monetary cure. It would seem as if measures that deal with the creation of "bank money" ought to be at least equally important.

Whether or not one sees our present troubles as primarily monetary in nature and origin—which I do not—it is obvious that the defects of our banking system have contributed greatly to the severity of the depression. And, whether or not money measures can be taken which will prevent future depressions, certainly better "bank money" than we have had in the past will make any future depressions much less painful.

In our survey of the first year of Roosevelt rule we have discussed briefly the banking measures that were taken.

In March all the banks were closed. Then they were re-opened under license, with the Government assuring the people that any bank so reopened was sound. That, as we have seen, involved making a lot of the banks sound, by subscribing to their capital structures so as to qualify them for the deposit guarantee plan.

As to the guarantee plan itself, in an address delivered before the Economic Club of New York on December 20, 1933, I said:

"I see no reason to change the opinion then expressed [in the previous June]. If a bank is to have an unknown liability, arising from whatever errors may be committed by other banks in all parts of the country, there ceases to be any sensible reason for owning the stock of such a bank, or in trying to run such a bank on sound, conservative principles. There is almost equally little sensible reason for trying to run a bank outside of the Federal Reserve System, although this may easily turn out to be the lesser of two evils.

"I believe, therefore, that the permanent guarantee provisions must at least be modified before they go into effect, so that, if banks must guarantee each other, they will at least know to what maximum amount in any one year they may be liable.

"I should hope that the entire guarantee provisions could be dropped when the banking system is properly reconstituted."

The Reserve City Bankers Association came out with a very full and carefully thought out analysis of the banking problem. When I saw the President in January, he seemed fairly well convinced that something had to be done before the permanent guarantee plan went into effect. A few weeks later he approved of postponing the decision as to the permanent plan, by extending the temporary plan beyond the date originally set for its expiration. The question is probably therefore no longer immediate, but it is none the less still to be solved.

In the same address from which I have just quoted, I went on to say:

"This country has suffered for generations from a hybrid banking system, with national banks under Federal control, and state banks under the control and operating under the laws of forty-eight different state authorities, in addition to partial supervision by the Federal Reserve. I can see no possible justification for the continuation of such a system.

"I can see no possible excuse for not bringing about a uniform banking system under uniform banking law, and under the control of uniformly operating authorities.

"If that is done, if branch banking is permitted to a reasonable extent, and if the minimum capital requirement for a bank is raised from the present ridiculous figure of $50,000 to let us say $500,000, I think most of our banking troubles will be over, the guarantee of deposits can be dropped, and the Government will soon be able to retire from its preferred stock investments.

"It would seem to me that a failure to act promptly along these lines during the next session of Congress may easily land the Government permanently in the banking business."

Except for the fact that the permanent guarantee plan will probably be postponed, there seems little likelihood that there will be any measures of banking reform put through at this session of Congress. Perhaps again it is undesirable for political reasons, about which I know nothing. Certainly I would be the last to advocate any hasty action. I should hate to see the banking problem tackled in the spirit in which the gold and currency problem was disposed of.

But until the problem is tackled, and tackled intelligently, there will be something radically wrong with our money mechanism—something that no amount of devaluation, or silver action, or currency experiments can cure.

It is not my intention to put forward here a detailed plan of suggested banking reform. Such a plan requires the collaboration of many minds and many hours of discussion. But along broad lines the problem is perfectly clear.

We have had private banking running more or less amuck under an inadequate and hybrid system of supervision. Because of this our banks have been creating "bank money" without due regard to the responsibility towards the community which this privilege entails. We know that we do not want such a system to continue.

What do we want?

There are a great number of people who are so disgusted with what they have had that they would like to see the Government step right in and do the banking business itself. For these people the steps already taken in that direction are only a beginning. I do not share their view.

I do not disagree with them just because I am a banker— being a banker is not such a great pleasure these days. I do not share their view because I do not believe that any government—least of all a political government such as ours —can render a banking service under which the nation's business can prosper.

I cannot picture banks run by political appointees supplying either the impartial integrity or the trained intelligence that we are looking for. Can you?

True enough, private bankers have not been so intelligent —some of them—nor so honest. One cannot legislate intelligence nor integrity. But one can provide an orderly uniform set of laws and regulations, and one can provide the machinery to see that they are obeyed. That is what we have never done. That is what we must do.

We must see that the same general rules apply to all bankers in all parts of the country.

We must see that bank officers are properly trained.

We must see that banks have adequate capital, and that the smaller communities are served by branches of strong banks, rather than by little banklets that go under in the first adverse wind that blows.

We must see that bank funds are invested to give the depositor maximum security, and we must make it possible for a bank that so invests its funds to earn a fair return for its shareholders. Otherwise there will be no capital for the banking business.

The soundness of a bank that earns too much should be

looked into just as quickly as the soundness of a bank that earns too little.

We must see that demand deposits are loaned out to finance turnover, and not capital transactions, so that "bank money" may always be what it is supposed to be—a medium of exchange.

We must build up the banking business as a profession and eliminate any tendency to make it a racket. To do that we must keep politics out of the banking business and let the courts be merciless in the enforcement of an intelligent banking law.

If we do not do these things, and do them soon, we shall inevitably suffer again as we have suffered in the past. We shall swing to the Left, and have government in banking —which means government in industry, commerce, agriculture, and all parts of our national life—a regimented society and the end of individual liberty. Or we shall drift aimlessly back to the Right and suffer once again the familiar abuses of our present system.

CHAPTER XXVI

The Investment Market—Kill or Cure?

As previously stated, the Glass-Steagall Act did accomplish one important element of banking reform:

It provided for a segregation of the commercial banking business from the investment business.

Under the terms of this law banks had to divorce themselves from their affiliates (by means of which they had circumvented the previous law) and leave the securities business altogether. Private banking houses were given the choice of giving up their deposit banking business or their securities business.

From the point of view of a necessary purification of the commercial banking business, this was a great step in advance.

From the point of view of the investment machinery—that is, the machinery by which capital accumulations flow into long-term investment in plant equipment and so forth —it was a destructive step, at least for the time being. But it was a destructive step which had to be taken, and without which the right machinery for the distribution of securities could never be set up.

We have seen in a previous chapter, "Capital and Credit," how necessary it is that there should constantly be an accumulation of savings out of income, in order that the machinery of production may be supplied with the fixed assets which it requires.

We have seen also that financing for such capital requirements must not come from "bank money," but should come from the "investment market."

The "investment market" is the place where savings out of income seek employment, and where business enterprises come to seek capital.

It is the function of the "investment banker" to guide savings into wise and profitable employment, and to guide business enterprise in obtaining the capital to which it is properly entitled, on favorable terms.

The capital, which comes to the investment market for employment, comes sometimes direct from the man who has accumulated it (the investor), sometimes through large groups of small accumulators—namely, the savings banks and life-insurance companies.

When the investment bankers lose their sense of proportion, as they did in selling foreign loans after the War, or when the public is seized by a speculative mania, as it was in 1927–29, the investment market ceases to fulfill its proper function and becomes nothing more than a gambling hell.

If, when this happens, the commercial banks are one and the same as the investment bankers, the whole "bank money" structure is affected, instead of just the capital market.

That is why segregation was necessary.

One of the things which had deeply impressed itself upon

the President's mind, long before he took office, was the iniquity of what had happened in the years leading up to the 1929 crash. One of the first things he wanted to do was to prevent a recurrence of such a speculative orgy. That was why the Securities Act was passed in such a hurry.

"I opposed this piece of legislation from the time when it was first drafted—not on grounds of principle, because I agreed with the principle. My criticism of the Securities Act is, in the first instance, that it does not go far enough, and, in the second instance, that it goes too far. . . .

"The framers of the legislation apparently attributed all past misfortune to only one cause—namely, the failure to disseminate to investors full and accurate information [concerning the securities they bought].

"In dealing with this one cause, they then went so far as to set up a series of penalties and liabilities which make the selling of securities practically impossible.

"I believe that the past misfortunes of investors have not been solely due to a lack of complete information as to the securities they bought. *There is such a thing in human nature as speculative greed, and I do not think it will ever be possible to legislate out of existence the desire to get something for nothing.*

"It is, however, possible, by proper legislation, to prevent the undue stimulation of such avarice, by making it more difficult to borrow on margin, and more difficult to obtain any loans for purely speculative purposes. In this respect the Securities Act does nothing whatsoever.

"Furthermore, the lack of uniformity in our corporation

laws—in fact, the absence of any Federal corporation law —seems to me to make almost inevitable the creation of unsound capital structures, and hence the sale of unsound securities to the public. Here again the Securities Act does nothing whatsoever.

"On the other hand, it appears to me to go much too far in treating the one cause of past misfortune with which it has concerned itself—namely, the dissemination of ample and accurate information. Under the guise of alleged identity with the British Companies' Act, it sets up a series of liabilities and penalties, which are neither well-defined nor reasonable, and which certainly bear no similarity to the British Companies' Act.

"These features will have to be amended if the investment market is to function.

"It has always seemed to me that this entire piece of legislation was pushed through with unnecessary haste and with unnecessary fanaticism. An atmosphere of emotion surrounded the whole question from the start, and anyone who dared to criticize was instantly accused of ignorance or self-interest."

That is from an address I made last December. I have nothing to add to it now. The Securities Act will have to be amended if we are to have an investment market.

Without an investment market it is hard to see where the necessary fixed assets of the production and transportation machinery are to be financed, unless by the Government.

Some of the President's advisers are of the opinion that

that is what should happen anyway. So it should—if we are going in for state capitalism.

But are we?

If one is to judge by the latest proposal for legislation in regard to the investment market, one must come to the conclusion that we are definitely headed towards state control of all industry, commerce, and transportation.

The "National Securities Exchange Act of 1934," introduced by Senator Fletcher on February 9, will, if it becomes law in its present form, go far beyond its avowed purpose of regulating the securities exchanges.

It does what the Securities Act failed to do with regard to margins and speculative loans in general—in fact, it does it with a vengeance. It prescribes various rules for dealers in securities and for officers of corporations whose securities are dealt in. A few of them seem good; some seem very bad—but:

It confers upon the Federal Trade Commission powers so extensive that the commission might, if it chose, dominate and actually control the management of every corporation whose securities are listed on a recognized exchange. It threatens our whole economic structure with the worst kind of bureaucratic interference and control. It has already been challenged as unconstitutional and attacked on any number of counts.

As I write this, the President's attitude toward the measure is unknown. He is on record as wanting some sort of bill regulating the stock exchanges passed at this session. He has not endorsed this particular proposal, but he has not opposed it either. By the time this book is published, whatever is going to happen will probably have happened, and I have a feeling that we shall not be any better off because of it.

More than sixty per cent of the unemployed are in the capital goods industries. Those are the industries which produce the fixed assets of production—iron and steel, building trades, machinery, etc.—as opposed to the industries that produce goods for consumption. These capital goods industries can never revive and re-employ their workers unless there is a capital market,—or unless the Government supplants the capital market.

That is why the Securities Act and the legislation now proposed concern far more than the investors or the investment bankers.

It looks very much as if the same atmosphere of fanatical reform, rather than of practical thinking towards recovery, which produced the Securities Act last April, is about to produce a second and even worse monstrosity.

Some day, when the professors have had their fling and when common-sense reasoning points to the necessity for a smoothly functioning investment system, I hope that we shall see such a system built up. Not along the old lines of high-pressure salesmanship—not upon the old principle of catering to the desire for speculative profit—but along the lines of careful selection practiced by a more educated public through the agency of more intelligently conscientious investment bankers.

Today we are moving in the direction of driving from

the banking business what few good bankers we still have. But the day will come—unless we change the whole basis of our economic philosophy—when investment banking will again be an honorable profession.

CHAPTER XXVII

Fish or Cut Bait

THE NATIONAL CREDIT

We have concerned ourselves so far with the soundness of our money mechanism, as represented by metal, paper currency, "bank money," and the capital issues, or investment market.

In the last analysis, the soundness of our money mechanism depends upon one thing alone—the integrity of our national credit.

When a government sets out to spend more money than it can ultimately repay out of bearable taxation, that government deliberately sets out to render void whatever constructive steps it may otherwise have taken.

National credit is not different from individual credit. If an individual borrows more than he can repay, he mortgages his future and that of his descendants—unless he prefers to lose his honor and resort to repudiation.

When a government resorts to excessive borrowing, it does precisely the same thing. It piles up taxation for future generations or else it prepares the way for repudiation.

Quite apart from any theories of deliberate currency debasement, such as the Committee for the Nation theory upon which the present Administration has embarked, the piling up of excessive national debt leads inevitably to printing-press money. And when that happens, there is no question of "controlled depreciation," or "reflation," or any of those nice-sounding words. When that happens, there is no stopping-place until you reach the bottom.

The bottom may be zero as it was in Germany—or in France after the inflation of 1789. Or it may be at twenty per cent of what used to be par, as it was in France after the Great War. That depends upon how much excessive spending and borrowing has been done. But wherever the bottom may be, you drop until you bounce on it.

The peak of our war debt was $26,594,267,000 in August 1919. By December 1930 this debt had been reduced to $16,026,086,000.

Since then the national debt has been steadily rising, until at the end of this fiscal year, on June 30, 1934, it will probably be in the neighborhood of $30,000,000,000.

By June 30, 1935 it probably will be about $32,000,000,000, and that is without taking into consideration some billions of indirect debt, such as Federal Farm Loan bonds, Home Loan bonds, and R.F.C. debentures.

In the fiscal year 1935–6 the budget is supposed to be balanced. The national debt should therefore show no further increase for that year.

I do not presume to know how large a national debt we can support. We have, in addition to the Federal debt, some nineteen billions of state and municipal debt. In all we shall have well over fifty billions, that we must retire out of taxation or repudiate. Some of the state and municipal debt doubtless will be scaled down (which is partial polite repudiation), but the bulk of the fifty billions will remain as a burden upon the taxpayer.

At this point let us dispel the widely held illusion that taxes can be levied upon a small part of the population and do not concern the great majority.

The wages of the many are paid out of the profits of the few. If you reduce the profits of business by increased taxation, you reduce the wages of the many. President Roosevelt himself said in a campaign speech in Pittsburgh, on October 19, 1932:

"Taxes are paid in the sweat of every man who labors, because they are a burden on production, and can be paid only by production. If excessive, they are reflected in idle factories, tax-sold farms, and hence in hordes of the hungry tramping the streets and seeking jobs in vain. Our workers may never see a tax bill, but they pay in deductions from wages, in increased cost of what they buy, or (as now) in broad cessation of employment."

Whatever the sum total of our federal, state, and municipal debt, direct and indirect, that sum must receive interest and ultimately be repaid by "the sweat of every man who labors."

How great that sum can become before taxation becomes unbearable, I do not know. I do know that there is a point somewhere beyond which we cannot go without the certainty of repudiation via the printing-press.

Probably, because of our great natural resources, the sum lies beyond the total we are scheduled to reach by June 1935.

But—are we going to stick to that schedule?

Broadly speaking, sticking to the schedule laid down in the President's recent Budget Message depends upon two things:

1. Whether we spend our money wisely, and
2. Whether we raise our money wisely.

Wise spending by the Government is spending to start private spending and so to eliminate the necessity for further outlays by the Government. Foolish spending is any spending beyond the ordinary cost of government that is not absolutely necessary for emergency relief or to start the wheels of private enterprise turning again.

Let us develop this a little further without going into too much detail, and let us look back for a moment at the chapter entitled: "What Roosevelt Inherited" (pages 81–84).

Relief, Recovery, and Reform. Those were the three main categories of Roosevelt's inheritance. In addition there was the problem of how to safeguard the national credit and yet bring its maximum force to bear upon the three major objectives.

What have we done in this latter respect?

For the unemployed we have provided various methods of emergency relief. That was right and necessary. We have tried to bring about permanent re-employment through the N.R.A. and Public Works.

The N.R.A. did bring about some increase of employment, but not nearly so much as was expected. Also it set in motion some currents which tend to decrease employment. That was because, while called the National Recovery Act, it was really not so much a measure of recovery as a measure of reform.

The N.R.A. cost, and is costing, a lot of money. Whether it is wise to spend that much money at this time on a measure of reform depends upon the wisdom of the reform and the necessity for it.

Then we decided to spend over three billion dollars on Public Works. Some of this expenditure will be represented by tangible Government-owned assets; some will not. Some of the tangible assets will even produce some revenue; others produce continuing expense.

But three billion dollars is an awful lot of money to spend in putting to work at most half a million men, and then only for a short time. (Some of the Public Works money was later transferred to the Civil Works Administration and used for relief work during the past winter. That has nothing to do with permanent employment.)

We have witnessed during recent weeks how difficult it will be to taper off the expenditures under the Civil Works relief program. Will it be any easier to taper off Public Works next year, as the schedule demands we should?

Lest this be considered destructive criticism, let me say that I have always felt that public works were a slow and uneconomical way of creating permanent re-employment. Much less money spent in direct stimulation of the heavy goods (capital goods) industries, where over sixty per cent of the unemployed are to be found, would to my mind have produced better and quicker results. There were several plans of this sort worked out last spring—notably by Fred

I. Kent and M. C. Rorty—which unfortunately fell into the discard.

So much for unemployment. Most of our money is being spent in relief or in making work at Government expense. Very little is being spent to start the wheels of private enterprise. Unless the wheels do start within the next twelve months, and start fast, it is difficult to see how our expenditure program will taper off on schedule.

To meet the agricultural problem we shall spend according to program about a billion and a half dollars. Of this amount one billion will come back in the shape of processing taxes (which I shall not explain because it goes too far afield). This billion does not, therefore, concern the budget, but it does concern the taxpayer.

We have also agreed to replace two billions of farm mortgages with Government-guaranteed bonds. That is part of the indirect debt over and above the $32,000,000,000 top that has been projected.

Whether these gigantic sums are being wisely spent, so that no further great expenditure on the agricultural problem will be necessary, I cannot judge. If further expenditure will be necessary, we shall not run on schedule.

Total loans and investments made by the R.F.C. and still outstanding total about three and a half billions. Many of these will be repaid. (Almost two billions of original loans have already been repaid.) Others will result in loss. How many more loans will the R.F.C. have to make?

How are the railroads and industries going to refinance their maturing bonds, with no capital issues market?

How is out-of-date and worn-out plant and equipment going to be financed, if the Securities Act remains unchanged and the Stock Exchange Bill becomes law?

It all comes back to the same question:

Are we spending our money so as to bring about private spending, and encouraging private enterprise to spend?

Or are we drifting more and more in the direction of letting the Government become the one great spender, the one great builder, and the one great employer of men and women? That is the meaning of the question:

Are we spending our money wisely?

And now for the second question, upon which depends, no less than the first, whether or not we run on schedule:

Are we raising our money wisely?

The answer to this question lies in the future. If we can maintain a sufficient degree of confidence in Government credit so that we can finance our requirements by selling long-term Government bonds to the people at a reasonably low rate of interest, then we shall be raising our money wisely.

If we cannot do this and have to sell excessive amounts of short-term Government paper to the banks, we shall be headed for trouble sooner or later.

An excessive short-term debt is only a prelude to printing-press money.

It may be that we shall be tempted—as other governments have been tempted—by the relatively cheap cost of short-term financing. That is what France did after the

War, with disastrous results to the French people.

It may be that we shall be driven to short-term financing by our inability to sell long-term bonds to the public. If that happens, it will be because the public is afraid that we are spending unwisely, or because our monetary experimentation has destroyed confidence in the future value of money.

Under the Gold Reserve Act the Secretary of the Treasury is empowered to use the two billion dollar stabilization fund, not only to stabilize the dollar, but to stabilize the national credit. That means that he can use the whole fund, if he likes, to buy U. S. Government bonds in the market and thus support an artificially high quotation for them.

I do not think for a moment that the Government would be so foolish as to attempt the financing of its huge requirements upon an artificially "rigged" market. To do that would be to do exactly what bankers have been justly criticized for doing in recent years. But the law does provide the possibility of that danger, as I pointed out in my testimony before the Senate Committee (see page 166).

There is another unknown factor:

As this is being written the House of Representatives has just voted overwhelmingly in favor of the Patman Bonus Bill, a measure calling for over two billion dollars of payments to veterans to be financed by the issuance of currency. This action was taken in the face of a clear statement by the President that he was opposed to any such measure.

The basic conception of our Government is that the

Executive should ask for appropriations and that Congress should grant them, or not, as it sees fit.

The basic conception is not that Congress should order the Executive to spend funds which he has not requested.

The unknown factor is to what extent Congress will abide by the President's program of expenditure, and to what extent it will attempt to increase this program by its own initiative.

Within the next twelve months, it seems to me, we must reach a vital decision.

Either we want our Government to help private enterprise back upon its feet, by careful assistance and intelligent co-operative planning—or we want our Government to supplant private enterprise altogether. If the former, we must run pretty much on schedule. If the latter, we must make up our minds to become a nation of regimented taxpayers—or else go bust.

Fish, or cut bait? Which shall it be?

CHAPTER XXVIII

Favorite Fallacies

PRICES, DEBTS, AND DEMAGOGUES

We are now very nearly ready to see, if we can, what really ails us.

I have indicated throughout this book that I do not believe our trouble is basically a money trouble. To be sure, we have money troubles—among others—and I have tried to show what some of them are:

We need an improved gold standard. We need an improved banking system. We need improved investment machinery. We need, above all else, a sound national credit. All these are part of the general money problem, which is important.

But our greatest trouble arises from our failure to realize that the money problem is not all-important, and from our consequent belief that we can find a monetary cure for our complicated ailment.

We make this mistake, I think, because our Government has fallen prey to two fundamental fallacies:

1. That a rise of prices is essential to recovery and can best be obtained by depreciating the currency, and

2. That the burden of debt is insupportable and must be relieved by depreciating the currency.

Before we proceed any further, it is necessary to pull

these two old favorites apart.

It seems to me that a *general* rise of prices is not essential to recovery.

What we want, after all, is an improved standard of living.

That means that we want the aggregate income of our people to be greater in relation to their aggregate cost of living.

A general rise of prices means a general increase of living costs. It follows that a general rise of prices, *unless it is accompanied by a corresponding rise of incomes,* reduces the standard of living still further.

Now, if you succeed in bringing about a general rise of prices by depreciating the currency, what have you done? You have raised living costs, but you have done nothing to raise incomes.

You have reduced the standard of living.

The avowed policy of our Government at the present time is to raise prices by depreciating the currency. This is being done in the vague and to my mind unjustified hope that only those prices will rise which we would like to see rise.

The Government hopes also to offset the increase in living costs by its various re-employment efforts, which are designed to raise the aggregate income.

The fallacy in this thinking is to my mind threefold:

1. What we really want is to raise those prices which have fallen disproportionately—farm prices are the out-

standing example. But, in order to raise them, we are adopting a method which in the end will raise all prices—and that leaves farm prices no better off than they were.

2. The Government seems to believe that it can offset higher living costs by ordaining that there shall be higher wages.

Higher wages can only be paid out of increased profits.

Increased profits can only come out of a larger volume of profitable business.

There can only be a larger volume of profitable business if "business" is freed from the fear of what may happen to the currency, what may happen to the banks, what may happen to the national credit, and what may happen to "business" itself.

3. Higher prices of all things—even if accompanied by increased incomes—are not necessarily desirable. In fact, it seems to me that lower prices for the necessities of life are desirable, if they can still be produced at a reasonable profit, by reason of greater volume.

Let us take an example: woollen socks. If woollen socks can be made cheaper, more people can afford to buy them, and more people will keep their feet warm. If more people buy them, the manufacturer can afford to take less profit per pair of socks, because his volume is greater. Because his volume is greater, he employs more labor, and that adds to the aggregate national income.

What is wrong with that? Why isn't it a good thing to increase volume by reducing cost, where it can be done profitably?

Our automobile industry has been built up on that principle, which was first recognized by Henry Ford.

I do not contend that this can be done with all things. Some things are selling below their lowest cost of production. In other cases there is no possibility of increasing volume by reducing cost. I doubt, for example, whether people would use more mustard on their roast beef if mustard were cheaper.

The conviction that you must cheer every time the price of anything goes up, and weep whenever anything goes down, is not very sound reasoning.

And now for the second fallacy.

The cry for "cheap money" in order to reduce the burden of debt has been heard throughout the ages. It arises from a fundamental failure to understand the very nature of debt, which is:

1. That for every debtor there must be a creditor,

2. That whatever the debtor gains the creditor loses, and

3. That creditors are everywhere more numerous than debtors; so that, when you do anything to help all debtors at the expense of all creditors, you are doing harm to the many for the good of the few.

That is what Bryan and his Populists failed to understand in 1896. That is what Senator Thomas, and Father Coughlin, and the Committee for the Nation fail, or refuse, to understand today.

Let us take a look at our debt structure, and see who owes what, and to whom.

The United States Government owes the holders of its obligations let us say,	$30,000,000,000
The states and municipalities owe holders of their obligations, let us say,	19,000,000,000
The railroads owe their banks and bondholders and other creditors	13,000,000,000
Corporations owe their banks and bondholders	35,000,000,000
City real-estate owners owe their mortgagees	35,000,000,000
Farmland-owners owe their mortgagees	9,000,000,000
Total funded debt (long-term)	$141,000,000,000
In addition:	
Banks owe their depositors about	$40,000,000,000
Life-insurance companies owe their policy-holders contingently about	$100,000,000,000

And there are various short-term debts concerning which not even approximate figures are available.

Exact figures do not exist, nor are they necessary for our purpose. What we are interested in are the big items that go to make up our "burden of debt."

What do these figures show us?

The debtors under the heading of long-term debts are:

1. The Federal, state, and municipal governments, for a percentage of 35%

2. The railroads,
   for a percentage of 9%
3. Corporations,
   for a percentage of 25%
4. City real-estate owners,
   for a percentage of 25%
5. Farmland-owners,
   for a percentage of... 6%

The creditors of the funded debt are:

The insurance companies.
The savings banks,
The commercial banks,
Hospital and educational endowment funds,
Trust funds and estates,
Other investors.

Under the heading of short-term debt, the debtors are:

The banks,
The savings banks,
The insurance companies,
Miscellaneous debtors.

The creditors are:

The bank depositors,
The savings-bank depositors,
The policy-holders,
Miscellaneous creditors.

Now, if we set out to "lighten the burden of debt" by debasing the currency, we do so, presumably, in the belief that we are helping the many at the expense of the few.

We do so because we are told by the demagogues that we must "free the poor people from the clutches of the wicked creditors."

Look over the list of debtors and creditors and see where you think the interests of the masses are to be found. See whether you find any justification for the argument.

There are over 68,000,000 life-insurance policies.

There are about 40,000,000 savings accounts.

The *bonds* of the governments, of the railroads, and of the corporations are held directly by the masses, or indirectly through the insurance companies, banks, savings banks, and charitable endowments. The rich holders are relatively very few. The *shares* of railroads and corporations, which would benefit through having their bonds partially wiped out, are owned very largely by the wealthy few.

So it comes down to mortgages and miscellaneous debtors.

The mortgages on city real estate are owed partly by the small home-owners. They should be given, and are being given, relief by moratoria and interest reductions, and by having the Government take over their mortgages from the present holders through the agency of the Home Owners Bank.

There are also a lot of mortgages on city real estate contracted by rich people and speculators.

On the other hand, the mortgagees—the people to whom
the mortgages are owed—are primarily the savings banks,
insurance companies, and charitable endowments—in
other words, the people.

Very much the same thing is true of farm mortgages. Farmers are being given relief through moratoria
and interest reductions, and through having their
mortgages taken over by the Federal Farm Loan organi-
zations.

Farm mortgages also are owned, as city real-estate mortgages are owned, by the people as a whole and not by the
wealthy few.

What is more, with all the talk about farm mortgage
distress, more than twenty-five per cent of all our farmers
have no mortgage debt at all. And another twenty-five per
cent of all the farmers have mortgages which are said to
amount to less than one fourth of the value of their farms.
(I cannot vouch for these figures, but they are commonly
accepted as correct.)

When we take our "debt burden" apart, is it not evident that the demagogues have been selling us a gold
brick?

Is it not evident that currency depreciation hurts the
masses so that a very small minority may be benefited?

But it goes further. The creditor class is even larger than
appears from an analysis of the "debt burden." (I keep using

these quotation-marks because the debt "burden" is also, as we have seen, the savings of the people.)

The creditor class includes millions of people who have neither saved nor borrowed.

The creditor class includes everyone who works for wages or a salary.

The factory-hand is a creditor of his employer every week, until he gets his Saturday pay envelope. The white-collar worker is a creditor, until he gets his fortnightly or monthly pay-check.

If the currency is depreciating, the purchasing power of wages is constantly diminishing. In time wages will be raised, but never as fast as their purchasing power diminishes. That has always been true, because employers must always be made to see the actual necessity for raising wages before they will raise them. Therefore there is always a lag between diminished purchasing power of wages and wage increases.

That is why every wage-earner suffers from a policy of "lightening the burden of debt by depreciating the currency."

And now, I hope, we have disposed of the second fallacy. It is a wicked fallacy, because it can be made so plausible.

Father Coughlin makes it plausible, with his talk of "bloody bonds."

Senator Thomas makes it plausible—to some—with his talk of transferring $200,000,000,000 to those "who owe the mass debts of the nation," from those "who did not earn it, do not deserve it, and must not retain it."

The Committee for the Nation makes it plausible, by talking about the restoration "of an honest dollar."

No one has ever explained why the 1926 dollar, selected by these people, is more "honest" than the dollar of any other particular year. The debts that are outstanding today were certainly not all contracted in 1926. Much of the long-term debt goes back much further. All of the short-term debt is much more recent. Why 1926? Why not 1913, for instance, before we indulged in all the inanities of the War and the post-war period?

Who says we should be better off with 1926 prices? And why? Look at a few articles that every housewife must buy:

	1933	1926	1913
1 yard of gingham	$.10	$.18	$.12
1 pair of cotton stockings	.25	.38	.24
1 ton of soft coal	6.75	7.25	3.75
1 pair of men's shoes	3.50	5.00	2.60
1 dozen fresh eggs	.261	.485	.345
1 quart of fresh milk	.106	.14	.089
1 pound of butter	.273	.531	.383
1 pound of bread	.071	.094	.056
1 pound of potatoes	.023	.049	.017
1 pound of coffee	.271	.510	.298

How do you like the "honest dollar" of 1926? If you are going to pay those prices, wouldn't you like to know where you are going to get a corresponding rise in income?

Do you see how the two fallacies go hand in hand? Do

you see why I say that our greatest trouble is our failure to realize that there cannot be a monetary cure for what ails us?

CHAPTER XXIX

What Really Ails Us

If, as I contend, our basic trouble is not a money trouble, then what is it?

In my opinion, it is no one thing, but a series of things:

In the first place, we have been on a physical, moral, and financial drunk, and we are suffering from a bad hangover.

In the second place, the spree has lasted so long that we have very nearly become habitual drunkards.

In the third place, we have started to go doctor crazy. Instead of realizing that what we need is to smoke less, drink less, and go to bed early for a while, we have taken to rushing about from doctor to doctor, complaining about our terrible headache, and asking for medicine to relieve it.

Finally, what with the drinking party, and the hangover, and the medicines we have swallowed, we really have made ourselves pretty sick.

Now let us see if we can get away from that not very attractive simile and state the same thing in more dignified language.

Until the War broke out, in 1914, the world was a fairly sensible and satisfactory place in which to live—at least so it seems as we look back upon it. Of course, the pre-war world must have contained a lot of evil—for one thing, it contained the seeds of war—but for our purposes I think we may consider the world of 1913 a fairly sober world, as judged by present-day standards.

Then Europe boiled over and we had war.

At first we stayed out, and contented ourselves with a policy of "watchful waiting." Supposedly we were neutral. Actually we were making money hand over fist out of supplying the Allies with foodstuffs and war materials.

That was where we first went wrong.

Had we joined the Allies at the start, that would have been one thing. Had we joined the Germans, that would have been another. Had we really remained neutral and refused to be lured by our pocketbook into a false position, that would have been a third honest alternative. But we did none of these things.

At practically the last minute we joined the Allies—not with an honest avowal of our reasons, which in truth were both mercenary and spiritual—but with a mouthful of words about "making the world safe for democracy." And because this maudlin phrase was born of war hysteria, nine out of ten honest citizens believed it.

Until then we had been a reasonably honest nation.

From there on we were honest neither with ourselves nor with others. Under a flag of "righteousness" we sent over our million doughboys, sold our billions of Liberty Loans, grew our billions of bushels and bales of wheat and cotton, planted our millions of surplus acres, erected our surplus plant capacity, and taught our people how to be profiteers, bootleggers, speculators, and gangsters, instead of honest, law-abiding, hard-working citizens.

That was how we got drunk.

Then we won the War and—because we were drunk—made the most ridiculously dizzy peace the world has ever known—a peace in many ways worse than a continuation of war.

Europe was bled white and bankrupt.

Unemployment had set in with the return of the armies to their homes. Social disorders threatened, and governments had no money with which to tide over distress.

New frontiers and new nations had disrupted the old channels of trade.

A new philosophy of national self-sufficiency had been born out of the bitter experience of war.

Religion, respect for law and order, and spiritual faith had given way to a new immorality—the immorality of disillusion and despair.

That is what we would have seen if we had had the courage really to look at it.

Had we looked at facts, we should have known then that our war debts from the Allies were uncollectible, because German Reparations were uncollectible.

We should have known then that the rest of the world would never again take the products of all our surplus acres and all our surplus plant capacity.

We should have known then that we ourselves faced a hard task of readjustment to the reduced demand for our farm products and our manufactured goods—a task that would involve the basic choice between national isolation and international rebuilding.

But we really saw none of these things. We took one look in 1919, shuddered, took a pull from the bottle, and decided it was all a horrid dream.

That was when we started in to become habitual drunkards.

For ten years thereafter we lived in a fool's paradise. We discovered for the first time the game of foreign lending.

"What?" we said, "You say Germany can't pay her Reparations? Nonsense! Why, we can lend her the money."

And we did.

And again: "What? Europe has no money with which to buy our exports? Rubbish! We can lend Europe all the money she needs."

And we did.

For a time it really looked as if we could beat the devil around the bush. If Europe did not borrow and buy from us fast enough, so that prices dropped a little, we borrowed and bought from ourselves. And prices went up again.

We had discovered the Midas touch. All we had to do was borrow and buy, and encourage others to borrow and buy. Then prices had to go up—that made profits go up—that justified higher prices—and that made the elevator boy a millionaire, and the banker a wizard of finance—and then—Ooomph!

But why bring that up? We all remember what happened from 1929 on. But—do we?

That was when we began to take medicines.

At first we took mild medicines, like bond pools to support bonds, stock pools to support shares, and wheat pools to support wheat. Because, of course, the break in prices was nothing but a "long overdue technical reaction."

Another favorite medicine consisted of encouraging statements from Big Business and from Washington. Usually, when these words of comfort came out, there was a renewed burst of liquidation!

That lasted for a year, and then our Central European loans and credits froze up tighter than a drum.

The slogan changed from "Borrow and buy" to "Sell and pay back"—only nobody could sell—or pay back.

Then England was forced off the gold standard. That was in September 1931. Other nations followed. Mysteriously, things began to look better abroad—and worse here.

Our banks began to buckle—then bend—then bust.

Prosperity seemed further than ever round the corner, and the people expressed their appreciation of Mr. Hoover's incantations in the election of 1932.

They wanted a new doctor and new medicine.

They got both.

In fact, they got more; for the new doctor turned out to be a surgeon as well as a medical man, and proceeded to perform a series of major and minor operations. What these were, in so far as they concern our subject, we have seen in the preceding chapters.

In some very important ways Mr. Roosevelt's medical and surgical treatments have gone straight to the root of our troubles.

He has cast out fear by his own fearless example. That is a great deal.

He has cast out bootlegging and gangsters, by amputating the Eighteenth Amendment, and is in a fair way to re-establish respect for the law.

He has brought to light the selfish immorality of the recent past and has inculcated a healthy amount of community-consciousness. He is making us realize that in a sense we are all there to serve each other—not only to grab what we can for ourselves.

All this is good, and it is perhaps more important than anything else that a President could do at this time.

On the other hand, in seeking to cure an infected toe, it seems to me that Dr. Roosevelt at times has come perilously close to amputating the whole leg.

In trying to raise farm prices and "lighten the burden of debt," he has depreciated the currency, which, as we have seen, hurts the great majority of the people and is of doubtful benefit even to the few.

In trying to cure the abuses of the investment system, he has for the moment very nearly eliminated it altogether.

In applying the pulmotor to the expiring banking system, he has had to provide the patient with a permanent night and day nurse—the R.F.C.—and he has not yet been able to perform the operation, without which the patient cannot hope to get well.

In trying to bring about re-employment, he has spent huge sums on relief and public works, which, if continued, will threaten the national credit.

And, in seeking to avoid this very danger to the national credit, he has tried to rehabilitate industry by means of the N.R.A. In so doing, he has given industry such a super-dose of strong medicine that it is at present gasping and gagging.

I shall not comment upon the agricultural program of production control, because, frankly, I do not fully understand it.

President Roosevelt has driven out one kind of fear, and let in another:

He has banished defeatism—that paralyzing terror, which prevents any action, lest it be wrong.

He has aroused the fear of too much medicine—too many operations—and too little chance for nature to do her share in the work of recovery.

One extreme begets another.

In the past we have left too much to nature—particularly to human nature. We worshipped wealth and became lawless and greedy.

That was wrong.

But it does not follow that we must rush headlong, past the middle ground of moderation, to the opposite extreme, where to earn an honest dollar is—as William Randolph Hearst has put it—"to be abused as a pickpocket."

It does not follow that, because we made stupid international loans, we should now be afraid to make productive investments in other countries—investments which would develop the undeveloped parts of the world, build up the volume of international trade, and tend to restore equilibrium in the balances of payment.

It does not follow that, because our banking system ran amuck under an outworn set of rules, we must cast out all bankers as "money-changers," and place the power to create money in the hands of a political machine.

It does not follow that, because we once worshipped the almighty dollar, we should now debase it—and fall upon our knees before the shrine of a price index.

Our social order is based upon two conflicting basic elements:

The rule of the survival of the fittest, and

The belief that all men are created equal.

Our economic system is a compromise, and will probably always be a compromise, between these two warring elements.

According to the first, we must have freedom of the individual, to seize and to hold whatever he wants and is strong enough to capture.

According to the second, we must love our neighbor, sacrifice the good of the individual to the good of the greatest number, and prevent the strong from profiting at the expense of the weak.

One, if you like, is the extreme of being the primitive man.

The other is the extreme of being completely civilized.

We are no longer primitive, but we are not yet completely civilized. That is why our economic order must represent a compromise. The Pagan and the true Christian are still at war within us.

That is why we have "maldistribution of wealth," which has nothing to do with the "money muddle."

So long as different people have different abilities, different desires, and different ambitions, it seems to me that we shall always have an uneven distribution of wealth, but it does not follow that we cannot do certain things to prevent or remedy excessive concentration in the hands of too small a number.

What *can* we do in that direction?

1. We can improve our system of taxation.

Tax-exempt securities nullify to a large extent the intended workings of the graduated surtax on large incomes. Secretary Morgenthau is fully aware of this and has urged the necessary action. Andrew Mellon urged it nearly thirteen years ago.

Beyond that, it seems to me that there should be a heavier tax on inherited investment income than on earned income so that the man who is rich because he had an industrious grandfather, pays more taxes than a man who derives the same income from being industrious himself.

2. In his recent article, "America Must Choose," Henry Wallace, Secretary of Agriculture, said:

"In the typical business breakdown, wealth tends to become more concentrated than ever. Creditors get more of the national income; debtors and wage-earners get less."

That has certainly been true of the present depression. And that is one contributory reason that the "burden of debt" has become so heavy.

Had it been up to me to meet the debt problem last

March, I should have given serious consideration to doing what the Australians did—instead of setting out, as we did, to depreciate the currency:

The Australians reduced the interest on all debts by government edict. (The amount of the reduction was a little less than twenty-five per cent.) In that way they lightened the burden of debt for the debtor, offset the tendency towards increased maldistribution of wealth, and preserved intact the sanctity of the principal.

(The fact that Australia also depreciated her currency has nothing to do with what I am here discussing. She depreciated her currency because she had to, not because of any theory.)

In other words, one can offset the tendency of a business depression to exaggerate maldistribution, by scaling down the wages paid to capital for a time.

Political abuse of this idea is of course possible. But it seems to me less dangerous than tampering with the currency, and far more direct in going straight at the heart of the debt problem.

I am not suggesting that we do this now.

We have had too much debt medicine already. It is an alternative to our present policy of currency debasement—not a supplement to it.

3. It seems to me that much could be accomplished in the desired direction by unemployment and old-age insurance.

Various plans of this sort have been worked out from time to time. The so-called "Dean Plan" seems to me one of the most interesting.

If all employers were compelled to pay a tax based upon an average of the man-hours of work done for them over a period of years, with a higher tax upon overtime hours, and

If, out of the proceeds of this tax, the Government would provide old-age pensions and unemployment insurance,

The result would be:

a. that profits of industries in boom years would be somewhat reduced—which would tend to dampen an excessive upward cycle and thereby make a violent depression less probable;

b. that, because of the higher tax on overtime, employers would tend to employ more workers for shorter hours;

c. that, as a depression set in, its progress would be slower, because purchasing power would decline less rapidly if the unemployed received insurance payments in place of wages;

d. that everyone who had been a conscientious worker would be assured of at least minimum support in old age. (This minimum pension can be increased by voluntary contribution of the workers.)

That is the sort of reform which, to my mind, will do more good than all the codes and Blue Eagles of the N.R.A.

But, again, it is an alternative.

You cannot ordain higher wages and shorter hours upon industry and then put on the suggested tax into the bargain. Nor is this a proposal which should be adopted in any case, without first subjecting it to the most acid test of the most intelligent criticism obtainable.

Finally, and quite apart from the distribution of wealth, we shall have to make up our minds whether to "go national or international," or to adopt a middle course.

Secretary Wallace has posed the two sides of this problem clearly and fairly:

"If we continue toward nationalism we must be prepared to make permanent the withdrawal from cultivation of over fifty million acres of fairly good farmland, and face the consequences of all the social and economic dislocations which are bound to ensue."

Or, alternatively:

"If, on the other hand, we choose not to put our agriculture under so high a degree of interior tension and discipline, we must drastically lower tariffs and reorganize industry, so that we can receive from abroad another billion dollars' worth of goods each year."

After analyzing what each course means, the Secretary comes to this tentative conclusion:

"The planned middle course I propose as a basis for present discussion is one precisely half-way between these two extremes: a line of march along which we would lower tariffs enough to bring in another half-billion dollars' worth of goods annually, and permanently retract of our good agricultural land some twenty-five million acres."

To my mind, complete economic nationalism is, practically speaking, an impossibility. Restriction of production and trade over a long period by various artificial means can only mean reduced standards of living and a return to economic swaddling-clothes.

A sensible middle course is clearly indicated.

Whether one feels as I do or not, it is a question of cardinal principle, which we should have faced and decided long ago. Certainly it should have been faced before we ever sat down at an international conference table.

It *must* be faced now.

Agriculture must face it, and realize that it must make sacrifice.

Industry must face it, and realize that it must forgo some of the protective pampering it has had in the past.

Labor must face it, for labor is the child and father of industry.

Capital must face it, and pay up for its failure to realize its responsibilities.

Above all, Government must face it, even if, in so doing, it loses some of its popularity.

Nature, in the shape of the business cycle, will help—in fact, is helping already. But Nature cannot do effective work so long as we are taking medicine.

There is no easy way out. But what has to be done can be done—and done cheerfully—

Not if we are ordered to go about it by a Government that tells us what to eat and when to go to bed . . .

But if we, as free people, will recognize the necessity for common sacrifice, stop talking about our headache—stop asking for medicine—get to work, and support self-government—instead of asking Government to support us . . .

Then it will not even seem very painful.

Who knows? We might recapture some of our lost pride in good craftsmanship, which once was added recompense, beyond our Saturday's pay. . . .

We might recapture a little of our lost leisure—our family life—and our forgotten pleasure in the little things. . . .

Who can tell?

We might even recapture our vanished faith.

APPENDIX

A. MODERNIZED GOLD STANDARD

B. MONETARY POLICY

C. NATIONALISM OR INTERNATIONALISM

A.

Modernized Gold Standard

1. First Open Letter to Senator Borah
(This letter was sent in answer to a public statement made by Senator Borah shortly after my address before the American Academy of Political and Social Science in Philadelphia on November 22, 1933.)

November 27, 1933

MY DEAR SENATOR BORAH,—

In your statement which appeared in yesterday's papers you said that, beyond criticizing the present monetary policy, I offered nothing constructive and simply advocated a return to the policy under which we arrived at our present disastrous condition. You also asked me what I had to offer to help the farmer. I welcome this challenge, because in my address the other night I could not do more than indicate an alternative policy, since the circumstances demanded that I should spend most of my allotted time in attacking the statements made by Professor Fisher and Senator Thomas. I did, however, state quite clearly that I favored "a reform of the gold standard."

Let me say at the outset that I have not attacked the present policies of direct farm relief through production control and credit extension. I am not an agricultural economist.

237

I am not even a monetary economist, but simply a practical banker, and I should be very foolish were I to venture into a field about which I admit that I know practically nothing. My address the other night touched upon the agricultural problem only to the extent that I said, and say again, that I think farmers are suffering from a disproportionately excessive fall of farm prices, rather than from a fall in the general price level; that if monetary manipulation can permanently raise the price level at all, it certainly cannot eliminate discrepancies; and that, in my opinion, the majority of farmers being more creditor than debtor, only a minority of farmers could gain by a controlled depreciation of the currency. I mentioned farmers only because I wanted to show that, apart from hurting all wage-earners, all holders of life insurance, all savings-bank depositors, pensioners, and bondholders, the present policy would harm a majority of that very group—namely, the farmers—whom it was primarily designed to help. Beyond that I cannot make any suggestion in regard to the agricultural problem, without stepping outside of the realm of things with which I feel fairly familiar. I can and do express full sympathy for distressed farmers, and subscribe to the necessity of solving their problem—but not at such a disproportionate cost to every worker who has lived or is living a prudent and thrifty life.

Permit me now to state as briefly as I can the immediate monetary actions that I think would be more conducive to recovery than our present policy, and permit me thereafter to amplify what I meant when I advocated the earliest possible return to a modernized gold standard. With regard to the latter, I think I can convince you that I am not simply urging a return to what we have had in the past.

Immediate Policy. I believe that no single action of our Government could contribute more effectively to recovery than the announcement of its intention to abandon further willful depreciation, to abandon the commodity dollar experiment, and to seek to bring about the early revaluation of the dollar in terms of a *modernized* gold standard. Such revaluation should not, in my judgment, be undertaken at once, and I do not pretend to know at what point between the present rate and the old par it should finally be. I do say, however, that an intelligent revaluation can best be undertaken in conjunction with similar action by Great Britain, which would of course involve the entire so-called Sterling Bloc. And I further venture the opinion that the best approach to such joint action would be an immediate arrangement for co-operative action by the Federal Reserve System and the Bank of England to limit excessive fluctuations of the two currencies in terms of each other. Without going into the mechanical details of such an arrangement, although I shall be glad to do so if you so desire, I should hope in this way, by trial and error, to find the point of natural equilibrium between these two currencies, which should then enable both nations to undertake final revaluation in terms of gold. The period of trial and error may take months or years, depending upon how rapidly order will come out of chaos on both sides of the Atlantic.

During this intermediate period I should expect that our people would be untroubled by fear as to the future of our monetary unit, because they would have, on the one hand, the assurance that our Government did not intend to seek any further depreciation, and on the other hand, the assurance that our currency would eventually be the kind of gold currency they could understand and trust. They would further be assured that, whatever point between the present rate of depreciation and the old par value of the dollar is ultimately to be chosen for revaluation, this point would be carefully determined and only fixed as a finality after it had shown itself to be consistent with the desired price level and other conditions of living.

Finally, as to immediate policy, I do not pretend to have sufficient knowledge to entitle me to an opinion in respect to Government expenditure and the Budget. I do not know how large a debt we can afford to run up. I do know that there is a point beyond which a sound monetary policy can be and will be rendered void by Government expenditure that cannot be supported by taxation. If we go beyond that point, we shall have paper money inflation, quite irrespective of monetary policy, but I have the greatest confidence in the Budget Director's vigilant awareness of that danger.

That brings me to the last question: namely, what do I mean by a modernized gold standard? I am sorry that some of our monetary theorists did not have the opportunity that I had to take part in the discussions of the "Gold

Committee" of the London Conference because I feel certain that they would have come away with the inescapable conclusion that international agreement on anything other than a modernized gold standard was quite out of the question. And I repeat what I said in Philadelphia, that it is inconceivable to me that any national currency system that we might adopt could work satisfactorily in the long run unless it were likewise accepted by a majority of other nations.

The two major criticisms levelled at the gold standard are, first, that a shortage or superabundance of gold may at any time upset economic conditions by causing an exaggerated rise or fall of prices; and, second, that the fiction of currencies redeemable in gold, to say nothing of bank deposits and securities indirectly redeemable in gold, is dangerous because it will always produce gold panics in times of depression. With this second criticism I thoroughly agree.

As to the first, I have found practically no one who fears a superabundance of gold and the consequent exaggerated rise of prices. The critics of the gold standard who attack it on these lines are almost uniform in their expression that what they fear is a shortage of gold and a consequent exaggerated fall in prices. No one has been able to prove to me that there is really a danger of gold shortage, but I am prepared to admit that so long as the fear exists, the mere existence of that fear constitutes a defect in the gold standard. How then meet it without resorting to untried currency schemes? Various things have been suggested. The basis of the propaganda for bimetallism, the basis of the theory of symmetalism, and likewise the basis of Professor Warren's theory, are a desire to emancipate prices from the influence of a possible gold shortage.

In so far as it is possible to make specific suggestions without knowing what will happen between the present time and the time when it will be feasible to reach international agreement for the re-establishment of an international gold standard, the following thoughts are suggested:

(1) Gold coin should be entirely withdrawn from circulation.

(2) The holding of monetary gold should be confined to central banks or banks of issue, who would use it for the settlement of international balances of payment resulting from temporary disequilibria in the foreign account, and who would likewise hold it as cover for their note issues.

(3) Note issues should be redeemable in gold bullion for export only, and shipments arising from such redemption should be made only between central banks or banks of issue. This suggestion involves overcoming French opposition towards giving up internal redemption in gold bullion. So long as any nation permits such redemption, hoarding of gold will be possible because anyone anywhere can buy exchange on that nation and then present currency and obtain gold.

(4) Gold miners should be compelled to offer their output to their respective monetary authorities and should only

sell to others for use in the industries, arts, and professions when permitted to do so by their respective monetary authorities and when the purchasers are duly licensed to buy.

It would seem further that under such a system: the legal *minimum* ratio of metal cover against note circulation might well be reduced to about 25 per cent. This applies only to countries like ours where there is such a ratio. Other countries, such as England, Sweden, or Japan, might agree to accomplish the same thing as a matter of practice, although no change in the law would be necessary.

These ideas were, as I have said, discussed in a preliminary way at the London Conference. They would require further discussion and proper modification before international agreement could or should be reached. I state them merely to illustrate how it would be perfectly possible to free the world from the spectre of gold scarcity and to free the central banks from the disturbing influence of a loss of gold due to hoarding. This is what I mean by modernization of the gold standard, which would meet the justifiable criticisms levelled against it without embarking upon new forms of money which, no matter how theoretically perfect they might be, could not possibly command universal confidence because they could not command universal understanding.

This brief statement would be incomplete if I did not add two further things:

First, that steps must be taken, no matter what international monetary standard is adopted, to provide for closer and more effective co-operation between the central banks or banks of issue of the various countries. This means that they must make more uniform and complete the statistical material and indices upon which they base their judgment. If they do this, and if they co-operate, there is no reason to assume that the familiar methods of contraction and expansion through central bank discount rates and open market operations will not prove amply effective in their control upon the short-term movements of capital. It should be stressed in this connection that central banks must use their powers of contraction in times of inordinate business expansion and not only their powers of expansion in times of depression. This is particularly true if, by economizing in the use of gold, we broaden the basis for a possible over-expansion of credit.

Second, apart from central bank control of normal domestic contraction and expansion, there must be an adequate and intelligent control of both long- and short-term foreign lending. It has been clearly shown that this cannot be left to the discretion of private bankers. Such control has been very effectively exercised by the Bank of England, through guidance rather than law or regulation. And such control must not, under any circumstances, take the form of exchange restrictions, which experience has shown serve only to stimulate the flow through illicit channels of the very transactions that they are designed to prohibit. No artificial barriers will prevent money from fleeing when it is afraid to remain, or from going where it hopes to find profitable employment. There is only one way to prevent an undesirable movement of capital, and that is to eliminate the reason for it. Remove fear—provide the reasonable hope of profitable employment—and capital will always show itself the most timorous of wanderers, the most comfortable and lazy of home-bodies.

As to the gold-buying program which we are now pursuing in our approach to a commodity dollar, let me say, first, that I believe neither in the theory nor in the practical method. Perhaps I am wrong. Perhaps the Warren theory, so ardently and so dogmatically proclaimed by the Committee for the Nation and others, has solved the problem that has puzzled economists for generations.

If, over a period of years, a superabundance of gold or a scarcity of gold should make itself manifest by exaggerating price trends, in spite of the precautionary reform that I have outlined (which I venture to doubt, because I for one do not believe that the quantity of gold plays any such direct and important part in a money structure such as ours),

Then I should be quite prepared to allow an international body endowed with supreme authority to alter the world price of gold—that is, the gold content of *all* the gold currencies—upwards or downwards from time to time, in order to offset the effect of gold shortage or superabundance, provided:

1. That I could see the remotest possibility of creating such an international body, not subject to political influence, and endowed with supreme power over the monetary authorities of the various countries, and

2. That I could assume that such a body would be furnished with complete and accurate information by all the various markets, and would use such information intelligently and impartially in reaching its conclusions.

I can see no reason to consider the creation and successful operation of such a body anything more than a Utopian dream, and I believe that to give the power of changing the gold content of the currency in each country to its own monetary authorities is fraught with the gravest danger. Furthermore, to do so would be to imply that the price level within any given country depends, not upon the world supply of gold, but upon the supply of gold within that country. That, to my mind, was the first implication of our present gold-buying policy, when our purchases were confined to operations within this country. The second implication, when we extended our purchases of gold to the world markets, was that we were setting out to raise the *world* price of gold; that is, to reduce the gold content, not only of our own currency, but of the currencies of other nations. If that is a correct interpretation, it implies acceptance of the belief in a gold shortage, acceptance of the underlying theory that the price level can be raised by counteracting a gold shortage through devaluation of all currencies, and it would seem to me that it implies the entirely unwarranted assumption that other nations will let us perform *our* experiment on *their* currencies. If that is not a correct interpretation, then the meaning of our present policy can only be that we consider the foreign exchange value of the dollar, particularly the sterling value, the important factor in determining our price level. That is not Professor Warren's view. It is, I think, the view of Professor Rogers. But here again, one is constrained to ask, why should other nations, particularly England, let us arrange things to suit ourselves? Professor Rogers, I feel sure, would agree that we can only accomplish our purpose—if that is our purpose—by international agreement and co-operation. And, I repeat, I can see no basis for expecting such agreement or co-operation along any other lines than an intelligent modernization of the gold standard. To this end I should like to see the labors of the London Gold Committee taken up where they were interrupted, at the earliest possible date.

I am sorry to burden you with so long a letter, but you quite justifiably asked for it, and, whether you agree with me or not, I trust that at least I shall have satisfied you that I am not just advocating "a return to the good old days."

Very sincerely yours,

JAMES P. WARBURG

THE HONORABLE WILLIAM E. BORAH,
    The United States Senate,
        Washington, D. C.

Senator Borah replied on November 30 with an open letter as follows:

UNITED STATES SENATE
Committee on Foreign Relations
November 30, 1933.

Mr. James P. Warburg,
No. 40 Wall Street,
New York City.
Dear Mr. Warburg:

I am in receipt of your communication under date of November 28th, in which you state your views touching the money question.

I am greatly interested in your discussion of this subject. It is refreshing to read a discussion of this subject without encountering a deluge of such terms as demagogues, dishonest dollar, cheap dollar, repudiation, communists, crooks and idiots. Your letter is a candid admission that the old orthodox system is obsolescent and the whole subject is open to fair discussion.

But I observe that your plan rests upon a proposed revaluation of the dollar in terms of a modernized gold standard, which, however, is not to be undertaken except in conjunction with similar action by Great Britain, which would, of course, as you say, involve the entire socalled sterling block. The possibility, to say nothing of the desirability, of such conjunctive action with Great Britain is so remote at this time, as I see it, that it removes any proposal based upon that fact beyond the realm of practical consideration and discussion. The entire history of Great Britain in money affairs, the repeated statements of Mr. Chamberlain in the last year and a half, the course which Great Britain has pursued and is now pursuing, the distinct conflict of interests of these two countries in the markets of the world, render remotely practicable any proposition based upon joint action with Great Britain. We can not wait, I venture to say, we will not wait, upon that event.

There is a further fact which I may be permitted to state, not in the way of criticism, but simply as the matter appears to me. I had supposed that the main criticism of the President's policy was based upon the element of uncertainty, the experimental period through which the President apparently feels the necessity of passing. Your proposition has many elements of uncertainty. It would seek to bring about the revaluation of the dollar in terms of a modernized gold standard. But such revaluation is not to be undertaken at once. It is not known at what point revaluation should take place. Such revaluation is not to take place until Great Britain cooperates. We can not know the effect of waiting upon such propositions. We can not know what the effect will be when it does take place. It is impossible to know what the effect would be upon the price level, although it seems to me it would be very unfortunate.

You are of the opinion we would have to go through a long period of trial and error, of months, perhaps years, and, in my opinion, of decades.

One of the great contributing causes to the present depression was the maldistribution of gold. Two nations with about one hundred seventy million population were in possession of something over 75% of the gold of the world. I do not see how your plan would remedy that situation in the slightest.

It does not seem to me that you contemplate dealing in any way with the question of silver in the Orient. The Governor of the Imperial Bank of India declared sometime ago: "The economists throughout the world are agreed that maldistribution of gold and over production of goods are two of the fundamental causes of the depression. If we consider the fact that the great masses of the Orient are half starved and less than half clad, one can not say that there is overproduction in terms of requirements but rather that there is overproduction in terms of purchasing power. Our job, then, is to recreate purchasing power, and we have the instrument at hand in silver, of which these masses are possessed. The remonetization of silver will furnish us with a needed purchasing power and will cause to disappear, through consumption, the world overproduction of goods."

Sir Henry Deterding makes the following statement: "Have the great bankers who depend on world-wide trading ever considered if it is possible for the world's trade to revive as long as about half the world's population—whose wealth is mainly in the shape of silver—are precluded from participating in the trade of the world by reason of the fact that the commodity in their possession has been artificially reduced in value to a point which practically prevents them from being buyers of anything?"

Leaving aside all questions as to the proper use to be made of silver in the monetary systems of the world, it seems perfectly evident that no monetary system can in the future be considered sound and efficient which does not restore to millions of people the money which they have used for three thousand years, which they desire to use, and which they will use if permitted to do so. The property loss incurred, the wide-spread misery entailed, by reason of taking away from eight hundred million people their only medium of exchange, their method of saving, was a selfish, brutal thing, having its origin in that blind greed which often works its own ruin.

Very respectfully,

[signed] WM. E. BORAH

To this I replied on December 1 with a second open letter:

December 1, 1933

DEAR SENATOR BORAH,—

I have your letter of November 30th, and it is most gratifying that, in spite of the missiles that are flying about on all sides, we are able to meet in a spirit of friendly and scientific discussion of the important money question.

You raise four points of criticism against my letter of November 28th:

(1) that I say revaluation can only be intelligently undertaken in co-operation with Great Britain, that such co-operation is unlikely, and that, therefore, the whole proposal becomes too remote;

(2) that I do not remove the much criticized uncertainty in monetary policy, largely because of the reason stated in (1);

(3) that nothing in my proposal would remedy the maldistribution of gold; and

(4) that in my proposal I left out the silver question entirely.

I shall give you briefly the best answers that I can to these four points.

(1) I venture to disagree with you as to the willingness of Great Britain and the Sterling Bloc to co-operate. I do not deny that there is a conflict of interest between them and us in many respects, but I believe that they realize that we have a mutual interest in establishing international monetary stability which far outweighs national considerations. I believe that the same is true of us, although we may not realize it. My reason for believing that such a willingness on the part of Great Britain exists is that I gathered this very distinct impression from direct contact with the various elements of the British Government; otherwise, I should not venture to take issue with you on this question.

It is, in any case, not difficult to ascertain whether my assumption is correct or not. I am quite prepared to say that if my assumption should prove wrong, and the British should be unwilling to co-operate upon a reasonable basis, I should then not advocate delaying our return to a modernized gold standard until their co-operation could be secured. I should then be in favor of doing the best job we could, either by ourselves or with the co-operation of such nations as might wish to co-operate. It may be that my training as an international banker leads me to exaggerate the necessity of international acceptance of a monetary standard in order that such a standard may be practically workable. I have subjected myself on this score to the severest self-criticism of which I am capable, but I still cannot escape the conclusion that if we revalue alone, we shall be subject to having our revaluation upset by the subsequent action of others. It is precisely for this reason that I think Great Britain would likewise be unwilling to revalue alone, but would be willing to revalue in co-operation with us.

(2) You say that my proposal does not eliminate uncertainty and you stress that you make this as an observation rather than a criticism. In part I admit the truth of this observation, but not in whole. We are suffering today from two kinds of uncertainty—uncertainty as to our ultimate monetary goal, and uncertainty as to the method by which we shall reach it and the time it will take to get there. By recommending abandonment of the present policy of willful depreciation and the ultimate aim of the commodity dollar, my proposal seeks to eliminate entirely the uncertainty as to what kind of money we are ultimately to have; it seeks further to eliminate much of the uncertainty as to how we are to reach this goal; but it quite frankly does not eliminate the uncertainty as to how long it will take us to get there or at what actual ratio we shall eventually stabilize. This residue of uncertainty, which I admit, is to my mind not only necessary but probably desirable, because I believe that hasty action might easily deny us the fruits of our long

and painful quest.

(3) I admit without reservation that there was nothing in my proposal of the 28th which would in itself redistribute the world's holdings of monetary gold. I agree with you that the present maldistribution must be corrected. In my opinion, the establishment of international monetary stability is a condition precedent to the redistribution of gold, but monetary stability will not by itself cause such redistribution. What then will cause it? The reduction and at least partial elimination of the present artificial barriers and restrictions to the free flow of trade between nations. If gold is to be redistributed, this can only be accomplished by international payment for goods and services, which is now rendered impossible by the network of tariffs, embargoes, import quotas, exchange restrictions, and other artificialities. I realize that this is highly controversial ground, but I must give you the only honest answer that I can give to an honest question. To avoid misunderstanding, let me add that this does not involve the necessity of removing all tariffs and other barriers of trade, but it does involve removing the superstructure of excessive restrictions, which have been superimposed upon what we had come to regard as the normal structure, by the various nations as a matter of national self-defense. I believe that here again the cure lies in international agreement rather than in the individual policy of any one nation, and I must stress that I cannot picture such international agreement unless there is first a more or less stable international monetary standard, because a depreciated currency will climb over the walls of

any tariff except an outright embargo.

(4) In my first draft of my letter of November 28th to you, I had included a paragraph on silver. I subsequently took it out because I was afraid that the mere mention of silver in a proposal to modernize the gold standard would lead to an exaggerated stress being laid upon that feature of it. I agree with you that the stabilization in terms of gold of a metal that is used for money by more than half of the world's population is a most important element in achieving international monetary stability. I do not go so far as to say that doubling the price of silver will double the purchasing power of the Chinese, because I believe that the purchasing power of the Chinese depends in the last analysis upon the goods and services that China can export. I do not know what level for silver is best for the development of the Chinese economy, but I do know that it cannot be good for the Chinese economy to have excessive fluctuations in the gold price of silver.

I know also that the gold price of silver has been depressed below what is probably its proper level by two arbitrary factors: the debasement of subsidiary coinages by many of the so-called gold countries and the decision to put India on a gold basis. I am in thorough sympathy with the projected international agreement between the major silver-producing countries and the major silver-using countries, particularly India, which would provide against excessive sales of silver on the world market during any given year, and which would also provide against the further debasement of subsidiary coinages and, if possible, for the ultimate remonetization of subsidiary coinages.

If such an agreement becomes an accomplished fact, I should be prepared to go even further in studying the possibilities of dignifying silver as a monetary metal by including it in some form in the gold family. This is not to be construed as opening the door to a consideration of bimetallism. It is not even to be considered as a suggestion that silver be used along with gold for the settlement of international balances of payment. What I have in mind is merely this: that some small part, let us say one fifth, of the metal cover required as legal minimum reserve against issue, might be allowed to consist optionally of gold or silver provided that a central bank, electing so to hold silver for a fifth of its metal cover, would carry it at or below a price to be agreed upon. In terms of my suggestion of November 28th, this would mean that if central banks must have a minimum of 25 per cent metal cover against their note circulation, four fifths of this metal cover must be in gold and one fifth may be in gold or optionally in silver if obtainable below the agreed price.

This proposal is very limited in value, its chief merit consisting in the creation of a stabilizing factor in that presumably central banks would be tempted to buy, if silver fell below the agreed price, and to sell if it rose above. I put forward the suggestion very tentatively in my testimony before the House Committee on Coinage, Weights and Measures in March 1932. I still put it forward in a purely tentative way because, frankly, I am apprehensive of saying anything that might be construed as support of those who would like to go much further in "doing something for silver."

Again I apologize for a long letter.

Faithfully yours,

JAMES P. WARBURG

THE HONORABLE WILLIAM E. BORAH,
The United States Senate,
Washington, D. C.

B.

Monetary Policy

1. The following is the general statement which I made to the House Committee on Coinage, Weights and Measures on January 18, 1934, before I had seen the Gold Reserve Bill as proposed. My comments on the bill itself have been included in the text in Chapter XXIII.

GENTLEMEN:

Your Chairman has asked me to prepare for you a discussion of the best move that the United States could make to end dislocations in the monetary systems. I understand that there have appeared before you during the last few days Dr. Sprague, Dr. James, Mr. Vanderlip, Father Coughlin, and Professor Fisher. I am, I think, fairly familiar with the views of all of these gentlemen.

In five published documents, dated November 22, 1933, November 27, 1933, December 1, 1933, December 20, 1933, and January 11, 1934, I have set forth rather fully my own views in regard to the monetary question. I have sent printed copies of each of these five documents to every member of both Houses of Congress. Not knowing how many of you gentlemen have done me the honor to peruse these papers, and being desirous of wasting as little of the

Committee's time as possible, I am somewhat at a loss whether to repeat briefly what I have previously said or to proceed from the assumption that the gentlemen of this Committee have been good enough to examine the documents I have sent them. I have therefore prepared a condensed version for the Committee, which, if it is your wish, I shall read to you, or which, if you prefer, I shall place on the record so that you can proceed at once to ask me any questions that you may desire.

I have not included in this condensation such statements as I have made concerning the banking and investment business, because I assume that those two problems lie outside the scope of your present inquiry. I must stress, however, that as the greatest part of our money is deposit money —that is, check money—the banking problem is closely related to this discussion.

Similarly, I have not touched upon the question of the budget and the present program of Government expenditure, but I desire to emphasize that the soundest monetary policy can and will be rendered void by an unsound Budget policy. I am not prepared to say how much we can afford to spend. A great deal depends upon the manner of spending it. I am prepared to say, however, that if we spend more than we can ultimately pay for out of taxation, we shall have paper money, in spite of any present resolve to the contrary. Whether we can accomplish our purpose without paper money depends upon whether we can sell a huge amount of Government bonds now, and later retire them; and whether we can sell Government bonds now depends in large measure on the removal of uncertainty in regard to the currency.

I present herewith the condensed statement, to which I have referred, and await your pleasure. Before proceeding to deal with it as you may direct, may I make the following general statement?

It seems to me that we have two major problems, and in regard to each of these two major problems we have, generally speaking, two major schools of thought.

The two problems are:

First. The relation of a monetary system to the general economic system, which means the relation of a monetary system to a depression, or to the recovery from a depression, and

Second. The kind of a monetary system that seems most desirable and adaptable to our needs.

In regard to the first problem, there is one school which says that the breakdown of the monetary system lies at the root of the whole economic depression. This school, to which Professor Fisher and Professor Warren belong, and to which Mr. Vanderlip belongs also, in a slightly modified degree, contends that since money was the primary cause of the depression, money must also be the primary means to recovery. The other school, to which Professor Sprague and Dr. James belong, and to which I also subscribe, holds that a depression is a complicated economic phenomenon and that recovery cannot be sought by anything so simple as a change in the monetary system. Furthermore, this school holds that whereas the breakdown of the monetary system undoubtedly added to the severity of the depression, the breakdown of the monetary system was in itself a result of the depression and not its primary cause.

My own reason for adhering to this belief is that I am convinced that the present depression arose primarily from the enormous expenditures for non-productive purposes which were brought about by the War. I believe that the dislocation of production, consumption, labor, and working capital was the consequence of millions of people changing over from their normal peace-time occupations into war-time occupations and, after the War, changing back again. I believe that all this placed a strain upon the monetary system which that system was unable to support, and that when the monetary system gave way it added to the existing confusion. It does not follow from this statement that I believe the monetary system which we had before the War should be the system to which we now seek a return. On the contrary, I believe that from the lessons of the last twenty years we can learn much which will help us to improve our money mechanism, and I have set forth in the documents to which I have referred what I believe some of these improvements might be.

When Professor Fisher says that there are only a handful of people who understand the mystery of money and that all our troubles have been due to the misunderstood "money illusion," he means, in effect, as you will doubtless have seen from his testimony, that prices expressed in money are the fundamental factor, and that cyclical booms and depressions could be avoided if we had a money with stable purchasing power, or—inversely expressed—if we had a stable price level. Neither Professor Fisher nor Professor Warren, nor any of the small select group that profess to understand the mystery of money, offer any real proof of this contention. They do not, for instance, explain how we were able to store up such a vast quantity of trouble for ourselves in the period of 1923–9, in spite of the fact that during that period we had, practically speaking, a stable price level. It is not pleasant to attack so eminent an authority as Professor Fisher by the means which I used in my address before the American Academy of Political Science, but, when an eminent authority makes a series of categorical assertions without offering proof, and merely states that those who disagree are ignorant and uninitiated into the mysteries, it is necessary to examine how true previous similar assertions of such an authority have shown themselves to be. I therefore felt justified in quoting a series of assertions made by Professor Fisher in 1929 which, in the light of subsequent developments, do not lead one to take his present-day pronouncements too seriously.

I am not an economist and I do not hold myself out as an authority on these matters. If the gentlemen of this Committee desire authentic refutation of the Fisher-Warren-Vanderlip school of thought, I would refer them to some very excellent short articles written by Professor Rufus Tucker, Professor Walter Spahr, Professor Edwin Kemmerer, and Dr. George Roberts.

Now, as to the second problem—namely, what kind of a monetary standard we should seek to establish. It follows quite naturally that the two schools of thought would seek a different mechanism, because they each have a different conception of what that mechanism is trying to accomplish. The Fisher-Warren school, to which Mr. Vanderlip formerly belonged but which he has recently more or less deserted in favor of a position considerably nearer to my own, desires a dollar of variable gold content, while Professor Sprague, Professor James, and I can see neither the necessity for, nor the practicability of, such a suggestion.

Your other witness, Reverend Charles E. Coughlin, belongs, so far as I can ascertain, to neither school. I have carefully studied his monetary proposal in a recent magazine article as well as the printed copies of his broadcasts. This study recently led me to address an open letter to Father Coughlin, which is the last of the five documents to which I have previously referred. After hearing him answer this letter over the radio last Sunday I still believe that Father Coughlin's proposal is based upon a number of fundamental misconceptions.

Apart from the theoretical merits or demerits of the Fisher-Warren commodity dollar idea, I do not believe in its practical value, because it presupposes that the same human beings who failed to manage the comparatively simple mechanism of the gold standard will be able successfully to manage a very much more complicated mechanism. Furthermore, no one knows better than the gentlemen of this Committee what happens to a highly technical and precise proposal when it is put through the Congressional machinery and turned into legislation, and none know better than the gentlemen of this Committee the pressure to which Governmental authorities are always subject from vociferous groups and special interest minorities.

It is always difficult for a government or a central bank to apply the brakes in times of over-expansion. It is always unpopular to attempt to check a boom, and as long as booms are unchecked we shall always have depressions to follow them. Think of the additional pressure that can be put upon those who would have to regulate, under the Fisher-Warren plan, not only the increase or decrease of the gold content of the dollar, but the selection of the commodities that are to compose the index, and the relative weighting of these commodities.

I have set forth in detail, in the documents to which I have referred, the concrete suggestions that I should like to make to the Committee in regard to the type of modernized gold standard that I think would best suit our requirements. With some of these proposals Mr. Vanderlip agrees. He has recently publicly expressed adherence to the reestablishment of a modernized gold standard, as opposed to the adoption of a dollar of variable gold content, which is advocated by his former associates on the Committee for the Nation.

Whereas the phrase used by the President last summer, "a dollar of constant purchasing and debt-paying power," seemed to imply a dollar of variable gold content, I think it is important to note that in his message in opening Congress he used words which do not necessarily imply any such thing. These words were: "a medium of exchange which will have over the years less variable purchasing and debt-paying power for our people than that of the past." These words represent a purpose with which I can and do declare myself in thorough sympathy. A modernized gold standard such as I have proposed would, I believe, give us a medium of exchange whose purchasing power would vary less over a period of years—considerably less—than under the old pre-war gold standard.

In his monetary message to Congress four days ago the President made three major recommendations; that all monetary gold be taken over by the Treasury; that the limits of revaluation be fixed between 50 per cent and 60 per cent of the old dollar; and that a large part of the profit due to revaluation be set aside as a fund to stabilize the dollar and the national credit.

I advocated an equalization fund as early as last March. I have always felt that any *"profit"* from devaluation should go to the Government.

When I returned from London at the end of July, I made a written report in which I stated: "The entire recovery program is jeopardized by uncertainty and doubt in the monetary field," and recommended, among other things:

> "That the United States Government should desire not later than October first to fix the amount of devaluation desired, in order to bring about the necessary adjustment of the price level, allowing for a subsequent variation of not over 10 per cent."

That is exactly what is now proposed. In July the range would have been 65 to 75 per cent, instead of 50 to 60 per cent. I thought then that a 30 per cent devaluation would be sufficient, and I still think that a devaluation of 40–50 per cent may work some injustice, and may store up future trouble, but I bow to the judgment of the President. He has listened to all sides, and weighed his decision with the greatest care. In any case I welcome the removal of the two extremes of uncertainty.

I am still in some doubt, after reading the message, whether the President intends ultimately to return to a fixed gold content or not. He has again used language which may easily, though not necessarily, mean a modernized gold standard, rather than a dollar of variable gold content. I deeply hope that it does.

There are still many dangers that beset our course. Some of them I have indicated. Others I prefer not to indicate, because I do not believe in looking for trouble, or in raising doubts, when I do not know all the factors that have been considered.

I feel, however, that we are now started in the right direction, away from uncertainty and towards a goal which will in time become definite, where today it is still somewhat enshrouded in mist. And I am profoundly convinced that, if you gentlemen will carefully analyze the experience of the past—if you will build upon that experience a monetary mechanism to carry out the President's high purpose—rather than starting out upon an entirely new conception of what money is, what money means, and what money can reasonably be expected to do, you will perform a service for which future generations will thank you—as I thank you now for this opportunity to present my views.

In addition to the general statement just quoted, I prepared for the committee a supplementary compilation of excerpts from previously published pamphlets, which I shall not include here, except for a special note on silver, which follows:

III. Additional Note on Silver for the Committee

It seems to me that silver has three aspects. It is a commodity. It is a medium of exchange. It is a basic monetary metal.

As a commodity it has been depressed by arbitrary curtailment of demand by governmental actions.[1] The proposed international agreement will seek to offset this by curtailing supply, and possibly will increase the demand, if subsidiary coinages are gradually remonetized.

As a medium of exchange it has the same relative importance as any foreign exchange unit; that is, its stability or instability affect the world economy much as the stability or instability of the Pound or Dollar or Florin affect it. In the silver countries it affects the internal economies of those countries, much as the dollar affects our economy, although some economies are much more sensitive than others.

As a basic monetary metal it takes the place of gold in

---

[1] Debasement of subsidiary coinages and putting India on a gold basis, thereby releasing her Treasury stocks of silver.

some countries, is used alongside of gold in others, and in still others is used only in subsidiary coinage or not at all.

———————

From the point of view of this inquiry,

1. As a commodity, it would seem that silver has recently received all the government help it can reasonably expect, as compared to other commodities.

2. As a medium of exchange, it would seem desirable that silver should be prevented from fluctuating excessively, just as it is desirable to prevent excessive fluctuations of the Pound or Franc or Dollar.

3. It is claimed that silver should be stabilized at a considerably higher price than it enjoys at present, "because this would increase the purchasing power of the silver countries." Why should it be good for China to raise her unit's value, if it is good for the United States to depreciate its dollar? If the gold countries want higher price levels, why should the silver countries want lower price levels? (Assuming that price levels can be raised or lowered in that way.) I have no opinion on what the right price would be.

4. As a basic monetary metal:

    a. It seems desirable to remonetize subsidiary coinages, provided the respective countries can make funds available under their budgets to buy the necessary silver.

    b. There is only one real argument for bimetallism or symmetallism, and that is based upon a shortage of monetary gold. If the economies in the use of gold which I have suggested are adopted, I do not believe there would be any shortage of gold.

5. Those who argue for silver money because they want cheaper money, might just as well argue for copper money, or iron money, or paper money.

C.

Nationalism or Internationalism

The Foreign Policy Association and the World Peace Foundation appointed a "committee on commercial policy" and asked this committee to prepare a report. The report was published in the first week in March. I was one of the sixteen members of this committee.

A summary of its report follows:

SUMMARY OF RECOMMENDATIONS

1. Tariff revision is an essential contribution to domestic recovery.

2. A new tariff policy should be based upon the interest of the nation as a whole. Such interest demands a foreign trade policy designed to bring about a more equitable and stable relationship between agriculture and industry. It also requires that foreign markets should be sought for those branches of agriculture and manufacture which can and should produce in excess of domestic requirements.

3. Since an increase of imports is essential to development of foreign trade, protection should be withdrawn from industries which, despite a long period of protection, provide only a small percentage of the requirements of American consumption, or in which the annual cost of protection is excessive in comparison to the value of their output.

4. The government should study the possibility of seasonal tariffs.

5. A new foreign trade policy must be such as to establish a sound equilibrium in our national balance of payments.

6. The tariff should be revised by means of reciprocity negotiations; but, in order to avoid the dangers of tariff bargaining, reciprocity should be employed only for the purpose of increasing trade.

7. The unconditional most-favored-nation clause should be retained with certain exceptions.

8. While Congress should define the principles of future tariff policy, it should delegate to the President the power to change tariffs, fix certain quotas, and conclude and put into effect reciprocity agreements.

9. The President should apply these principles only after investigation and report by a reorganized Tariff Commission or other administrative body.

10. Future tariff reduction should take into consideration the extent to which import trade has been handicapped by depreciated currency.

11. The development of international trade depends upon the conclusion of an international currency agreement.

12. Exchange controls can be removed only when creditor countries resume purchase of goods from debtor countries. Once the United States commits itself to this position, it may be desirable to convert "frozen" credits into long-term loans.

13. While it is desirable to resume international lending under certain conditions, there is danger in the widespread extension of export credits before the government has developed a sound commercial policy.

Mr. LaFollette makes the following reservation: "I cannot join in all recommendations as to Foreign Trade Procedure. There are other expressions I do not agree with. It is essential to restore the volume of exchange of goods and services, foreign and domestic. The measures recommended are generally sound as immediate steps."

Mr. Soule makes the following reservation: "The measures here recommended are desirable as immediate steps. As long, however, as our internal economy is not socially planned and controlled, there will be grave danger that any type of foreign trade regulation will be carried out in such a way as not to conform with the basic policy which the committee approves. Tariffs may be adjusted or quotas may be set so as to favor special interests, to the detriment of the needs of the people as a whole, when the authority rests with Presidents and Commissions as well as when it rests with Congress. It should also be pointed out that if our internal production were socially planned and controlled, the best solution of the foreign trade problem would be in some form of government monopoly, which would obviate all necessity for such clumsy expedients as tariffs or quotas."

Mr. Warburg makes the reservation to Recommendation No. 11 that "the development of international trade depends on the re-establishment of an international monetary standard and currency stability."

Index

i

A NOTE ON THE TYPE
IN WHICH THIS BOOK IS SET

DEVICE OF
ROBERT GRANJON

This book is set in Granjon, a type named in compliment to ROBERT GRANJON, *but neither a copy of a classic face nor an entirely original creation. George W. Jones drew the basic design for this type from classic sources, but deviated from his model to profit by the intervening centuries of experience and progress. This type is based primarily upon the type used by Claude Garamond (1510-61) in his beautiful French books, and more closely resembles Garamond's own than do any of the various modern types that bear his name.*

Of Robert Granjon nothing is known before 1545, except that he had begun his career as type-cutter in 1523. The boldest and most original designer of his time, he was one of the first to practise the trade of type-founder apart from that of printer. Between 1549 and 1551 he printed a number of books in Paris, also continuing as type-cutter. By 1557 he was settled in Lyons and had married Antoinette Salamon, whose father, Bernard, was an artist associated with Jean de Tournes. Between 1557 and 1562 Granjon printed about twenty books in types designed by himself, following, after the fashion of the day, the cursive handwriting of the time. These types, usually known as "caractères de civilité," he himself called "lettres françaises," as especially appropriate to his own country. He was granted a monopoly of these types for ten years, but they were soon copied. Granjon appears to have lived in Antwerp for a time, but was at Lyons in 1575 and 1577, and for the next decade at Rome, working for the Vatican and Medici presses, his work consisting largely in cutting exotic types. Towards the end of his life he may have returned to live in Paris, where he died in 1590.

This book was composed, printed, and bound by H. Wolff Estate, New York. The paper was manufactured by S. D. Warren Co., Boston.